WEIRD MUSIC THAT GOES ON FOREVER

A PUNK'S GUIDE TO LOVING JAZZ

BOB SUREN

ILLUSTRATED BY BRIAN WALSBY

FOREWORD BY PAUL MAHERN

INTRODUCTION BY LUCKY LEHRER

Microcosm Publishing
Portland, Ore | Cleveland, Ohio

WEIRD MUSIC THAT GOES ON FOREVER: A Punk's Guide to Loving Jazz

© Bob Suren, 2024

First edition - 3,000 copies - March 26, 2024

ISBN 9781648412080

This is Microcosm #922

Edited by Olivia Rollins
Cover and design by Joe Biel
This edition © Microcosm Publishing, 2024
For a catalog, write or visit:
Microcosm Publishing
2752 N Williams Ave.
Portland, OR 97227

www.Microcosm.Pub

All the news that's fit to print at **www.Microcosm.Pub/Newsletter**

www.Microcosm.Pub/Jazz

To join the ranks of high-class stores that feature Microcosm titles, talk to your rep: In the U.S. **COMO** (Atlantic), **ABRAHAM** (Midwest), **BOB BARNETT** (Texas, Arkansas, Oklahoma, Louisiana), **IMPRINT** (Pacific), **TURNAROUND** (Europe), **UTP/MANDA** (Canada), **NEWSOUTH** (Australia/New Zealand), **OBSERVATOIRE** (Africa, Middle East, Europe), **Yvonne Chau** (Southeast Asia), **HARPERCOLLINS** (India), **EVEREST/B.K. Agency** (China), **TIM BURLAND** (Japan/Korea), and **FAIRE** and **EMERALD** in the gift trade.

Did you know that you can buy our books directly from us at sliding scale rates? Support a small, independent publisher and pay less than Amazon's price at **www.Microcosm.Pub**.

Global labor conditions are bad, and our roots in industrial Cleveland in the '70s and '80s made us appreciate the need to treat workers right. Therefore, our books are MADE IN THE USA.

Library of Congress Cataloging-in-Publication Data
    Names: Suren, Bob, author.
    Title: Weird music that goes on forever : a punk's guide to loving jazz / by Bob Suren.
    Description: Portland : Microcosm Publishing, 2024. | Summary: "Once you've
        collected every 7" from your favorite label, broken your back in the mosh pit, and
        become so well-versed in the interpersonal dynamics of every hardcore band that
        there's nothing more to learn, what's a punk to do? Try jazz, recommends Bob Suren.
        No, really. Suren, who wrote Crate Digger about his life and work in punk, turns his
        obsessive gaze onto another form of rebellious, improvisational outsider music, but
        this time with more sax"-- Provided by publisher.
    Identifiers: LCCN 2023050204 | ISBN 9781648412080 (trade paperback)
    Subjects: LCSH: Jazz--History and criticism. | Jazz--Analysis, appreciation. | Jazz
        musicians.
    Classification: LCC ML3506 .S935 2024 | DDC 781.65--dc23/eng/20231025
    LC record available at https://lccn.loc.gov/2023050204

MICROCOSM · PUBLISHING

Microcosm Publishing is Portland's most diversified publishing house and distributor, with a focus on the colorful, authentic, and empowering. Our books and zines have put your power in your hands since 1996, equipping readers to make positive changes in their lives and in the world around them. Microcosm emphasizes skill-building, showing hidden histories, and fostering creativity through challenging conventional publishing wisdom with books and bookettes about DIY skills, food, bicycling, gender, self-care, and social justice. What was once a distro and record label started by Joe Biel in a drafty bedroom was determined to be *Publishers Weekly*'s fastest-growing publisher of 2022 and #3 in 2023, and is now among the oldest independent publishing houses in Portland, OR, and Cleveland, OH. We are a politically moderate, centrist publisher in a world that has inched to the right for the past 80 years.

TABLE OF CONTENTS

PART TWO: NOTABLE ARTISTS AND SELECT RECORDINGS • 50

FOREWORD

Paul Mahern

Frank Zappa once joked that jazz was the music of unemployment. He certainly could have been talking about punk rock.

I am endlessly dedicated to the promotion of music. Music has been my life's consistent motivator (playing it, listening to it, and talking about it). The opportunity to say a few words here at the beginning of this beautiful celebration of music is an honor.

For me, all music that is not European classical is folk music. If regular people tell their truth through sonic vibrations, it's folk. I understand it is a broad definition, and most don't share this point of view. But the more we subdivide, the greater the chance we will miss something that could ultimately be very important to us. Unfortunately, many music fans live in a bubble of their creation. I was fortunate to grow up in record stores full of cantankerous clerks who were always willing to tell me what I should be listening to. This information from wise elders was a welcome shortcut to finding the gold. I now teach two courses in music history at the Jacobs School of Music at Indiana University, and the sole reason I do this is to help young people hear music they might not get to experience otherwise.

Bob Suren has done a fantastic job researching and efficiently covering much ground here. His heart-centered approach feels like the music itself. Furthermore, Brian Walsby's drawings bring the music to life like a killer collection of baseball cards for basketball fans. No one in this book, including the creators, was motivated by capitalism, which is pure punk. It takes a lot of love to undertake a project like this, and I am incredibly grateful.

When listening to early acoustic process jazz records (before 1927), it is essential to understand that what we hear is a modified and limited representation of what the bands sounded like in a live setting. Because of recording limitations, song arrangements were heavily edited in length. Drums were challenging to capture, and because of that, they were often absent. As Bob points out, jazz was outsider music even in those early days. It was wild, raucous, and free teenage sex music. Since the big record companies like Columbia made classical recordings, it was up to small independent labels like Gennett and Black Swan to record and promote this new heathen style of music. Jazz, like punk, spread worldwide because of the efforts of independent labels.

Furthermore, those early records acted as antiracist propaganda. Long before rock and roll, jazz was played by Black and white people together onstage. The Benny Goodman Band was integrated by 1938.

When the microgroove LP came along in the late 1940s, jazz musicians utilized this more extraordinary landscape to their advantage. In 1962, Rudy Van Gelder started recording all the Blue Note sessions in stereo, while pop music productions remained focused on singles and mono for years. Thus, jazz is the original album format.

I am certainly not some creepy nationalist, but if I were, I would point to jazz as one of the primary reasons that it was important for America to exist. So, I suggest you read this book, put on some Dolphy, and smash the fucking state.

Paul Mahern

Bloomington, Indiana

September 11, 2023

INTRODUCTION

Lucky Lehrer

Perhaps you've picked up this book because for you, jazz is a revelatory art form. You've made the pilgrimage to Blue Note in New York, and Miles Davis's *Bitches Brew* happily cohabits in your music collection with the Sex Pistols' *Never Mind the Bollocks*. However, if you've never learned to appreciate jazz, you may find yourself listening to Miles Davis's classic jazz recording "So What" and literally thinking, "So what?" This may be especially true if the music you most relate to is punk. Maybe you perceive jazz musicians as mild-mannered mannequins and associate their music with the sonic haze of the bourgeoisie. If you're honest, you might also admit that the reason you've ignored jazz until now is that you "just don't get it." To appreciate the power and complexity of jazz requires learning something about its particular language and socio-historical development. This includes, as Bob Suren's well-researched and provocative book points out, the unique ways that punk and jazz intersect.

In *Weird Music That Goes On Forever: A Punk's Guide to Loving Jazz*, Suren connects two seemingly disparate genres and, in the page-turning process, hips readers to amazing, timeless music. If you grew up with "999" handwritten on a pair of dirty white high-tops and a tape of the Damned in your cassette player, Bob's book will introduce you to dozens of musicians you may have otherwise missed from an art form that's as American as the Ramones.

Subgenres such as hardcore, post-punk, noise rock, glam punk, pop punk, and grunge all have counterparts in jazz. The seminal punk band the MC5 worked songs by Ray Charles, Screamin' Jay Hawkins, and Pharoah Sanders into their set. Lou Reed credits Ornette Coleman as a major influence. In fact, Don Cherry, a member of Coleman's jazz band, even performed with Lou Reed. Saxophone solos on the Stooges' "Fun House," X-Ray Spex's "Identity," and Fear's "New York's Alright If You Like Saxophones" have clear jazz overtones. The common jazz practice of "trading fours" was aggressively used in the Circle Jerks' song "Red Tape."

I observed in *Forbidden Beat: Perspectives on Punk Drumming* that great bands have good drummers. Jazz is no exception. As a young drummer, I'd put on headphones and play along to Buddy Rich's *Big Swing Face* LP. At a speedy 123 beats per minute, the band's ferocious rendition of the Cole Porter classic "Love for Sale" is much remembered. Each solo builds under the strength and precision of explosive drumming. When Jay Corre reaches his solo's second go-around, his tenor violently scats percussive ostinatos that are as exhilarating as anything recorded on vinyl. The intensity of Buddy Rich's jazz band left an indelible impression that I instinctively imported to punk.

As a listener, a deeper appreciation of music helps you find the answer when a new song inevitably leads to the question: "I like this tune, but why?" I recommend allowing Suren to challenge what you imagine music can or should be. Use this book to deepen and refine your listening skills. Was that a trumpet or a flugelhorn solo? Is the bass player using a standup or an electric bass? Is the drummer using sticks or brushes? See if you can learn to tell the difference. This is not an academic exercise! Your love of music multiplies when you invite your ear to listen more intently and discern each player's contribution to the combined sound.

Going one step further: Does the song follow the formula of verse, verse, chorus, bridge verse or a different structure? Is the music you're hearing associated with a particular musical genre? Do you hear elements of other genres as well? Do you like the way the instrumentalists and vocalists perform? You may like what you hear, or you may notice imperfections. Do the lyrics focus on imagery or figurative language and rhyme? Jazz performances, like punk, are often one-off, semi-improvised conversations between players and audience.

There are more overlaps between jazz and punk. Early jazz performers were dismissed as amateurs, not dissimilar to punk musicians. Like many punk players, they were accused of lacking the ability to play "real" music. Critics famously shunned jazz's first practitioners. Jazz, like punk, was considered rebellious. The few performance venues that existed were dimly lit, gin-soaked hellholes. Moreover, several legendary jazz performers, including Miles Davis, Charlie Parker, Chet Baker, Thelonious Monk, and others, were iconoclasts who clashed with the law and spent time in jail for their behavior. Many punk rockers can relate. Jazz, like punk, challenged musical and social authority, ultimately upending ossified forms, and expanded conventional notions of music.

Inspired by the modest goal of penning a primer for those otherwise unfamiliar with jazz, Suren delivers an approachable treatise that broadened my appreciation of jazz. This book is a wonderfully entertaining survey, spotlighting some of the best jazz music, its luminaries, and its pioneers. Welcome to songs where your ears and heart ecstatically align . . . music that beckons you to listen and play in ways you may have never imagined.

Lucky Lehrer

West Hollywood, California

September 15, 2023

THE SCENE

*T*magine, if you will, a crowded room—perhaps a basement—full of chatter, coming from the coolest-looking people, all there for a common love of a music that most people (fucking squares) just do not get. You must be in the know just to know about this place. Maybe you saw a poster at the top-secret record shop, or maybe a fellow enthusiast clued you in. Whatever. You're there.

The band takes the low stage under poor light, four bad cats, and just blows the lid off the goddamn place. They slaughter the stage. The audience is inches away, rapt. Everyone is sweating. As soon as one song ends, the next starts. Seamless. Inspired. Wild. Music for the outré crowd. You know this is where you belong. You know this is your life.

Ramones at CBGB? Bad Brains at Madam's Organ? The Bags at the Masque? Blatz at Gilman?

No. This is jazz.

Why Jazz? Why Me? Why? Why? Why? But Why?

y now you're probably saying, "Why would I want to listen to jazz? I have all the Discharge 7-inches. What else do I need, fuckface?"

Well, maybe you want to broaden your palate a bit. Maybe you're bored with songs about Reagan and nuclear war. Maybe you're feeling adventurous and want to hear music the likes of which you've never heard before. Maybe you don't want to tell your Tinder date that the last record you bought was by a group called Herpes Alpert and the Tijuana Ass. And just maybe you're starting to look silly in tight black jeans and a Shitlickers shirt with the sleeves cut off. Maybe you'd look great in a porkpie hat!

Jazz and punk have a lot in common. Both started in the underground, largely performed by marginalized people. Jazz musicians were abusing drugs before Sid Vicious was even born. And while artists of each genre have been accused of "selling out," both styles are still, in their purest form, very unpopular. And that. Is. Cool.

Classic punk bands like Black Flag, the Clash, Bad Brains, and more have all been influenced by jazz. Spit Stix from Fear, Lucky Lehrer from the Circle Jerks, Bob Weber from Really Red, and Al Schvitz from MDC were all jazz drummers before getting into punk. Those awesome drum fills in "Red Tape"? Jazz. West Virginia's number one punk band, Th' Inbred? Jazz. The entire *Process of Weeding Out* album? Jazz. "We've Got a Bigger Problem Now"? Jazz!

See? You already have a little jazz under your studded belt. Now, let's cook, man!

How I Became a Punk Rock Jazz Cat

hen I first heard jazz, I said, "This is weird music that goes on forever." But now I say, "This is weird music that goes on forever!" Same words, different inflection.

I got into jazz late in life, in my early 40s. Unlike punk rock, which I got into in 1983 when I was 14 and tossed myself into for decades, I wasn't there for jazz. I never saw any of the jazz greats. (I did see the Ramones and the Dead Boys!) I have been to present-day jazz clubs, but that is a sad scene. It's like a Civil War reenactment but with more walking bass lines. At least the ones I have seen.

I didn't pick up any of the essentials while they were hot off the press, like I did with every 7 Seconds record. I didn't send well-concealed cash to Blue Note Records, the way I did with Dischord and Subterranean. I didn't write letters to Cab Calloway. (I did write letters to Kevin Seconds—even if he never wrote back.) Most of my favorite jazz musicians died years before I checked out their albums.

I guess jazz had always been around me, in movies like *Bullitt* and TV shows like *Get Smart* and *Mission Impossible* and *Frasier*, but I don't think I knew it was called jazz. The first time I remember trying to listen to jazz was in 1999 with a CD copy of the Miles Davis album *Birth of the Cool*. And I thought, "I don't get it."

Maybe 10 years later, I heard the Charlie Parker CD *Jazz 'Round Midnight* and I thought, "Wow! I love this!" It just clicked that day. I guess my tastes had expanded without me knowing it, or I had had my fill of three-chord punk outrage. By then, Charlie Parker had been dead for more than 50 years, but I didn't know that. I went scampering back to that copy of *Birth of the Cool*. I was ready for Miles. And perhaps fittingly so, as Charlie Parker was the one who gave Miles Davis his start in jazz.

"What else sounds like this?" I wondered.

The Brandon Regional Library in Brandon, Florida, was the next step in my jazz quest. The library was within walking distance of my record store, Sound Idea—an all-punk record store, mind you.

By the time I "got" jazz, the store had been closed a year or two. But from 1995 to 2008, I carried vinyl and CDs of punk bands from all over the world, from the Ruts to Rupture, from the Adverts to Agathocles, from the Buzzcocks to Bluttat, but no jazz. Or anything else.

In fact, I was unabashedly rude to people who came in looking for, say, Bruce Springsteen or the soundtrack to *The Lion King*. A description of my shop, in a newspaper article about local record stores, read, "Now here's a store that doesn't bother with customer arse kissing. It's punk rock or SOD OFF!" My go-to record to get annoying normies out of the store was the first one by Anarchus, a Mexican grindcore band that sounds rather similar to a school bus plunging off a cliff and landing on a dynamite factory. I still love that record.

Anyhow, the Brandon Regional Library had an amazing collection of jazz CDs. And you were allowed to check out 50 CDs at a time. Fifty! It was overwhelming, just as it had been in 1983 when someone handed me a mix tape with Crass, Agent Orange, Minutemen, Gun Club, Bad Brains, the Freeze, D.O.A., and 20-odd more. Too, too, too much information at once—but dizzying in a sublime way. GIMME GIMME GIMME!

Just as when I'd started buying punk rock records 30 years earlier, I didn't know what to get. I just picked up records that looked like they'd be good. Teenage punk me used to memorize the lyric sheets and thanks lists of bands like Dead Kennedys, Minor Threat, Scared Straight, and Pillsbury Hardcore for guidance—what to be on the lookout for. With the jazz CDs from the library, I started scanning liner notes and recording credits, cramming my brain with names like Max Roach, John Coltrane, and Herbie Hancock. If those guys had anything to do with a record, you knew it would be good. Holy shit, was I ever late to the jazz party, but good music has no expiration date.

How I Wrote This Book and How to Use It

No doubt a lot of deeply serious jazz lovers and musicians will say, "USE IT LIKE TOILET PAPER!" And their opinions should be weighed. I'm not a jazz expert, I am just a guy who started digging on this music less than 20 years ago. In jazz terms, I am a newbie and a nothing. (Jazz people, like punks, tend to measure each other by "time in the scene" and what music they know. So, yes, there is a bit of thinly veiled snobbery involved.) I tried to write this book like an enthusiastic friend who wants to turn you on to some great music and make the baffling terrain of sound easier to navigate, just as a handful of older punks eased me into the punk scene with mix tapes and loaned zines. Consider this a friendly starting point from your punk rock uncle. There are far more complete jazz history books on the jazz history book market, available in jazz history bookstores around the world (but mostly in France), which you should read later on. But I should mention that none of those jazz history books compare Ella Fitzgerald to Roach Motel.

The book is split into two parts. Part One is a bare-bones history. Much of my base research comes from the primary sources: the recordings. Over the years and as I got more and more of the music under my belt, I decided to dig deeper by picking up jazz history books, biographies, and autobiographies, which helped me put the music I was listening to into a historical context. Many of these titles are mentioned throughout the book, and you'll find a suggested reading list at the end. And there are several excellent documentaries and movies available online, which also are mentioned throughout.

Part Two is a handful of biographical sketches about some of the most important artists of the genre. A lot of the biographical information we have about the jazz artists themselves has been collected from fuzzy memories or 10th-generation retellings of events. Some of the artists seem to contradict themselves or to be unclear on their own histories: Chet Baker, Art Blakey, and Billie Holiday were all unreliable narrators. When I think a particular detail or event should be taken with a grain of salt, it will be clear to the reader. And while my chronology is as ordered as it can be, I couldn't always nail down exact dates.

When I needed colorful quotes and anecdotes, I turned to the internet, where I scoured record reviews, interviews, essays, obituaries, and videos. You always hear people say, "Don't read the comments," but I did read the comments and that improved the research, often sending me on side trips that yielded richer details or contrasting opinions. And holy shit, do jazz people have a lot of long-winded opinions. Some of their online jousting makes the tired "Does *Earth A.D.* suck?" punk debate seem charming.

The biographical sketches are presented in alphabetical order by last name, just as if you were browsing through a record store. I have made an effort to get the historical information to you in a digestible form, so I did a lot of streamlining. Many important artists are not mentioned at all, and the biographies are condensed (even the extra-long one on Miles Davis, believe it or not—the comprehensive Miles Davis story would be hundreds of pages).

I conclude each biography with a list of suggested listening material by each artist. These are my personal choices, culled from my personal archive, that I think make good ice breakers. I listed them in chronological order—because I am not a barbarian—but you can listen to them in any order you like.

As for the book, my advice is to read it all the way through, in order. At the very least, I suggest reading Part One to orient yourself within the long, multi-branched evolution of jazz. Then you could use Part Two to learn more about any of the artists that have piqued your interest. But they're all interesting, so eventually you're going to want to read it all. I have read this thing all the way through, from beginning to end, about nine times at this point and I can tell you it takes about eight and a half hours. There are some plucky footnotes, too. Only poseurs skip the footnotes.

PART ONE:
A HISTORY LESSON WITH PUNCHLINES

What Is Up with That Crazy Name, Daddy-o?

*T*guess a good thing to address right off the bat is the word "jazz." The definition of jazz has been debated, as has the definition of punk. I guess you can say, "I know it when I hear it." Even the etymology of the word has been debated. But one colorful theory, which you may find in the *Historical Dictionary of American Slang*, is very dirty and thus of interest to scum like you.

When this new music started taking shape in turn-of-the-century New Orleans, there was no name for it. The exciting new style, played mostly by Black people, derived largely from West African folk music but also incorporated elements of then-current European popular music and classical. People immediately began associating this peppery new music with *fucking*!

The Creole dialect morphed "orgasm" into "jasm," and people started saying things like (and here I am paraphrasing, in a Creole dialect, no less), "Whooo—eee! That new music makes me feel like I'm gonna JASM!" "Jasm" was shortened to "jass," and the new moniker stuck like, uh—something very dirty!

In fact, what is considered the very first jazz record was released in early 1917, by a group called the Original Dixieland Jass Band. The two-song 78-rpm record was a huge hit and the new style spread like herpes all over the world. Paris was especially taken by these herpetic new tunes. (Ironically, everybody who played on the first jazz record was a white guy. It was not the last time white people would be accused of appropriating the music. But at least they were *cool* white guys. An article in *Smithsonian Magazine* says of the Original Dixieland Jass Band, "Like punk rockers 70 years later, its group members gleefully proclaimed their outsider status in the musical world.")

And at some point, "jass" became "jazz," from which we get the modern "jizz" or "jism." So, I guess you could say that it *came* full circle.

And then there are some other boring theories, but why would you want to hear those?

Women in Jazz, Women in Punk, Rhubarb Pie, the Wrecks Demo

Over the decades, both punk and jazz have undergone major changes in gender representation. Compared to early jazz, early punk rock had a lot more women onstage, including Poly Styrene of X-Ray Spex, Penelope Houston of the Avengers, Alice Bag of the Bags, Exene Cervenka of X, and Nyna Crawford of VKTMS. Then there were the female bassists, practically mandatory in the 1970s, like Gaye Black of the Adverts, Lorna Doom of the Germs, Dianne Chai of the Alley Cats, and Patricia Morrison, who played in the Damned, the Gun Club, and Sisters of Mercy. And let us not forget guitarist Poison Ivy Rorschach of the Cramps and drummer Karla "Mad Dog" Barrett of the Controllers. Women were well represented in punk's first decade.

I got into punk in 1983, the tail end of first-wave hardcore. I didn't get to witness the early days of punk or the evolutionary years, approximately 1978–1980, when punk got faster, meaner, shorter, and perhaps dumber. But from what I have read and from what I have gathered talking to older punks, the more aggressive scene that emerged during the gestation of hardcore didn't appeal to a lot of women, and their numbers dwindled. By the early 1980s, one didn't see a lot of women onstage. Of course, there are some notable exceptions, like the badasses Mish Bondage, Donna Damage, Kira Roessler, Greta Brinkman, and Lisa Nash; Fort Lauderdale's mostly female Morbid Opera; and all four members of the Wrecks.[1]

The 1990s saw the riot grrrl movement, with groups like Bikini Kill and Spitboy drawing attention. Leading crust bands like Nausea, Antischism, Damad, Monuments To Ruins, and Kylesa had female vocalists, providing encouragement for other women to form bands. Women were back onstage and back in the recording studios in numbers even greater than in the 1970s. And this trend has extended to the present. I would venture to say that the present-day global punk scene is in all ways the most diverse it has ever been.

Women's representation in jazz has followed a slightly different trajectory. The timeframe of this book is approximately the first 80 years of jazz. And during that timeframe, the people onstage and in the studio were primarily Black and primarily male. Besides a few vocalists and the occasional pianist, there just weren't many women on the bandstand during the years of our discussion. Judging from some of the anecdotes and interviews I have stumbled across, the formative jazz era was a hyper-competitive boys' club, full of rivalries, bathroom humor, atomic wedgies, and the occasional stabbing. The two biggest women in jazz were the vocalists Billie Holiday and Ella Fitzgerald, who

---

1 Allow me this tangent because I love the band so much: The Wrecks' 1982 demo is one of the finest demos ever recorded. It's all attitude. In fact, one of the songs is called "Punk Is an Attitude." The Wrecks could be considered proto riot grrrl. And the whole demo should have been a record. It could still happen. Just one song appeared on a compilation. The other eight have remained largely unheard. Around 2014, I wanted to do something about that, so I made a video and posted it on YouTube with all of the songs. The *Dangerous Minds* blog heard about the video and posted a link. The video got about 3,000 hits in one day. Aaaaand . . . one of the Wrecks is the sister of our hero, Kevin Seconds!

will be discussed in depth in Part Two. We'll also discuss Alice Coltrane, who wasn't a big name but who made exotic music and had an interesting life.

I don't know what the deal was with jazz and the lack of women artists. My guess is that the traditions and mores of the time kept women at home baking rhubarb pies and not touring the world, shooting heroin, and getting herpes. Keep in mind that women weren't even allowed to vote in the Land of the Free until 1920, the Dixieland jazz era, and even then getting herpes was frowned upon.

An older jazz expert I talked to about this said the formative years of jazz were not particularly welcoming to women. Billie Holiday was fired once or twice for "being difficult," which is probably more of a reflection of the sexism of the times than her professional demeanor. But one female artist who was always treated with respect was Ella Fitzgerald. Her male contemporaries always spoke of her with love and awe. Even Sinatra respected Fitzgerald. By the end of the 1960s, the U.S. had become more progressive and so had jazz. In the late 1960s and 1970s, female artists like Alice Coltrane and Linda Sharrock got a little more of the spotlight.

Another factor to consider is how jazz history has been recorded. *DownBeat Magazine*, the main publication of jazz since 1934, has traditionally been staffed by men, who knowingly or not may have excluded females in their coverage. (A look at their website today does show more diversity.) And out of all the books I have read about jazz, none of them were written by women. But if you do a deep dive into jazz history, you will notice a trend. There were lots of women behind the scenes, like the intriguing Baroness Pannonica de Koenigswarter, Nellie Smith, and Helen Moore, who figure largely into the picture but aren't mentioned in those brainy liner notes on album covers. These were women who provided financial support, emotional support, hot food, and health care to major jazz artists who might have otherwise succumbed to homelessness, malnutrition, disease, and prison. There are also some great parents in the history of jazz, whose support was crucial to the success of artists like Miles Davis, Eric Dolphy, and Duke Ellington.

The good news is there are many women playing jazz today, including the successful pianist Diana Krall (who happens to be married to Elvis Costello), saxophonist Melissa Aldana, and vocalist Cyrille Aimée. Jazz may have started apolitically, but by the mid-1950s, the civil rights era, the most daring artists were expressing their dissatisfaction with life in America. With that in mind, it's good to see jazz continuing to evolve to be more inclusive.

Dixieland and D.R.I.

*T*hat early jazz from 1917 New Orleans, Dixieland jazz, was kind of corny but it was a start. A lot of the early groups were based around banjo or upright piano, which—face it—are not the coolest instruments in the world. But a cool thing started happening in the 1920s as these bands got recorded and put on shellac, the predecessor to vinyl records.

Improvisational playing is the defining feature of jazz. (Dark sunglasses being third on the list.) Every player in every group wanted a chance to step into the spotlight and show off a little. But the 78-rpm format has a playing time of about five minutes per side. So, to make sure every member could get a moment to fucking go off, the bands started playing faster.

A punk rock parallel could be found in the tale of the first Dirty Rotten Imbeciles record, an unprecedented 22-song 7-inch record. How did Houston's number one hardcore group get twenty-fucking-two songs on a 7-inch record? They played fast as fucking shit—and launched a million bands who adored them, including Montreal's vastly underappreciated Capitalist Alienation, Fresno's Plaid Retina, and Stockholm's Mob 47.[2]

---

2 Word is that when Minor Threat played Houston on their 1983 tour, one of the Dirty Rotten Imbeciles tried to sell a copy of their debut vinyl to an unimpressed Ian MacKaye, who told them no thank you, adding that any record with that many songs must sound like shit. Mr. MacKaye was correct in one respect. Nearly 17 minutes of music crammed onto a 7-inch did greatly diminish the sound quality (but not the playing!), and not long after, D.R.I. were forced to agree with him and reissued their twenty-fucking-two-song landmark as a 12-inch record, with better sound quality and a bigger picture of the guy with the fucked-up haircut on the cover. By the way, the guy with the fucked-up haircut on the cover was the original drummer and the haircut in question was known as a "mange head," in the parlance of early '80s H-Town punk.

Big Bands, Swing, a Kevin Seconds Joke

But we were talking about jazz. Jazz kept evolving. While the early New Orleans jazz was often in the form of marching bands, by the 1920s, the bands began to sit down. Maybe because they got so big. This was the era of orchestral jazz, also known as symphonic jazz or big bands.

And they were literally big bands, orchestras of 10, 15, or more, who made light-hearted, romantic dance music, which became known as swing around 1930. Some of the household names from this popular era are pianist and composer Count Basie, vibraphonist Lionel Hampton, and drummer Gene Krupa, as well as vocalists Ella Fitzgerald, Billie Holiday, and of course Frank Sinatra, who was also known as the Erotic Trench Coat and the Capo of Cannoli.

My favorite artist from this era is the prolific composer and pianist Duke Ellington. You may have heard the old saying that Kevin Seconds has written more songs than Duke Ellington and Adam Sandler combined. And if you haven't heard it, we've probably never met. I say that all the time. It may even be true.

Some hair splitters like to differentiate between so-called "hard" swing like Count Basie and "sweet" swing like Benny Goodman, but it's all swing. Do punk rockers ever split hairs? All the fucking time. I used to have one guy who would buy hundreds of dollars of records from me at a shot—but only in the then-popular powerviolence niche. I had another guy who wouldn't buy anything recorded after 1983. They were exhausting customers.

Anyhow, the original-original jazz people did not get this big-band swing stuff at all. To them it was, at best, a curiosity. Some of them got on board and others just faded away into irrelevance.

For about half a decade, swing was kind of underground, with scattered clusters of dedicated fans, ignored by the normies.

But by around 1936, swing broke and became very popular. By 1942, Frank Sinatra was the superstar of swing, possibly because he had blue eyes, which were in vogue at the time. And swing remained the most popular style of Western music until the birth of rock and roll. (Which Mr. Sinatra hated—big surprise. By the way, Frank Sinatra was born on December 12, 1915; he emerged from the womb a fully formed middle-aged man, drinking a martini.)

Swing Dies, Jazz Gets Faster, and Bands Get Smaller

ut more than a decade before Elvis Presley made swing seem old, dull, and pompous, it began a slow, painful death. What caused the demise of swing? As with most things in life, there were multiple factors.

A big blow to big bands came in the form of the musicians' strike that began in 1942. For two years, members of the American Federation of Musicians went on strike against record labels for unfair royalty payments. Most professional musicians belonged to the union and stood with each other in solidarity, causing an almost-complete stoppage of new records for a couple of years.

But due to a union loophole, vocalists were not subject to the same terms of the strike. Record labels took advantage of this and started releasing vocal-oriented records with scant instrumentation provided by non-union musicians. The era of the pop vocalist emerged, and leading the way was the Uncle from Hoboken, the Chairman of the Elks Lodge, the Colitis Kid, the New Jersey Turnpike, Old Flop Sweat, Francis Albert "I COULD HAVE YOU KILLED" Sinatra.

Meanwhile, a lot of the people playing in the big bands got drafted or volunteered for service in World War II. One volunteer was the enormously popular bandleader Glenn Miller. In 1942, the 38-year-old Miller gave up his $20,000-a-week salary to entertain the troops in the European Theater with a whopping 45-piece orchestra. Sadly, on December 15, 1944, a plane Miller was on went down somewhere between England and France. Not a single trace of the plane nor passengers has ever been found. The disappearance of Glenn Miller remains one of aviation's greatest mysteries.

Also in 1944, to raise money for war efforts, the U.S. federal government passed the cabaret tax, a flat 30-percent-off-the-top tax on clubs that featured live music. It was a huge blow to jazz clubs. Some closed. Others managed to survive by employing smaller bands.

These small, lean bands started playing a faster style with more emphasis on rhythm (BOOM! BANG!) than melody (WHOA! WHOA!). Jazz became more intense and cerebral. You might find this sliver of time analogous to those few transitional years circa 1978–1980 when punk rock grew a tumor called hardcore.

But the final nail in swing's coffin was that the style was played out. Teenagers didn't want to listen to their parents' music. This is where jazz starts to get interesting to me.

Bebop, Kansas City, Charlie Parker, and Heroin

*B*ebop, or just bop, the faster, harder, busier, more complex style played by smaller groups, allowed the musicians to be more creative with tempos, rhythms, and song structure. (Bebop gets its name from a vocal approximation of the style's terse, short notes.)

It is "musician's music," made for listening, not for dancing. As opposed to the more structured swing style, bebop groups have a general idea of where the song is going and an agreed-upon melody (called "the head" in jazz talk), but they give each member a chance to step into the spotlight for a solo. And they really try to squeeze in as many notes as possible during each solo. Improvisation, the beating heart of jazz.

The capital of bebop was Kansas City, Missouri. It has been said that jazz was born in New Orleans, but it grew up in Kansas City. But why there?

By the late 1930s, Kansas City was a literal crossroads of commerce and culture. If you were traveling across the country, you probably had to stop in KC. It was also known to be a city with loose liquor laws and all kinds of vices. It has been said that during the bebop era you could get heroin and herpes on the same street corner in Kansas City—and still have enough money in your pocket for a slice of rhubarb pie, a cup of coffee, and a movie with two cartoons and a newsreel.

Clubs were open virtually around the clock, thanks in large part to Thomas Joseph Pendergast, a political boss who only briefly held public office but pretty much ran the city—until he was imprisoned for tax evasion. But by then Kansas City was a modern-day Gomorrah. Yay!

Bebop formed out of a variety of influences and the super-competitive club scene in Kansas City. The patron saint of bebop is Charlie Parker, known as "Yardbird" or "Bird," who began playing sax at age 11. He wasn't great at first, and he was once so embarrassed onstage that he virtually disappeared for a year to practice, up to 15 hours a day. When Parker reappeared on the scene, he was a new player. He was phenomenal. And he was a junkie. Sadly, Parker is largely credited with introducing jazz to heroin.

Parker's peer group assumed heroin was the secret to his prowess and soon dove into the shit themselves. The heroin myth has endured for decades, plaguing music scenes around the world. In fact, a jazz musician I met in October 2018 who had played with Miles Davis, Chet Baker, and Charles Mingus, among others, said to me, "Heroin really does make you play better! It just ruins every other aspect of your life."

In any case, the bebop era, roughly the early 1940s to mid-1950s, is when the jazz story—and the music—really starts getting exciting, and Charlie Parker was the king. Many of the players who passed through his band went on to even greater acclaim and monetary reward, such as drummer Max Roach, pianist Bud Powell, trumpet player Dizzy Gillespie, and the baddest motherfucker who ever took the stage (sorry, Iggy), Miles Davis.

The 1950s, Cool Jazz, and Herpes Distress

*F*azz music is full of irony, and perhaps the greatest irony is that during what was probably its most productive era, the 1950s, jazz shrank in popularity.

Of course, if you cared about popularity, you probably would never have gotten into punk in the first place and you probably wouldn't be spending your evenings and weekends hunting for obscure demos from the former Yugoslavia, by the likes of U.B.R., Tožibabe, and Herpes Distress. So, welcome to jazz, you goddamn mutant! Gabba, gabba, we accept you, one of us!

Rock and roll is the oft-cited culprit in the slaying of jazz. But there were other factors, too, like television, a new way for people to spend their leisure time. And ironically again, jazz helped kill off its own audience when many musicians switched from the fun, high-tension, 145-beats-per-minute, frenetic bebop style to what became known as cool jazz, a smoother, slower, smoldering, smoky style that embraced the "less is more" philosophy. Young people didn't want relaxing, sophisticated music, and who could blame them?

After the bebop revolution, jazz branched off into new subgenres. And the lines between subgenres could be blurry. They often overlapped chronologically and musicians tended to straddle two or more types of jazz. Miles Davis, for example, was a major player in five or six subgenres of jazz over several decades.

The 1950s were an especially fruitful time for jazz, even if the audience was smaller. Record labels like Blue Note, Columbia, and Prestige were the Dischord, SST, and Alternative Tentacles of jazz, releasing some of the best-loved, best-selling, and best-sounding albums. Their logos are symbols of quality.

Some people argue that the best year for punk was 1979. Others say that it was 1981. Or 1983. Or whatever. Most jazz fans, including me, will point to 1959 as the best year for jazz. In fact, there is a fantastic BBC documentary called *1959: The Year That Changed Jazz*. (It is easy to find online and offers a wealth of information.)

The documentary tells the story of four landmark jazz albums: Charles Mingus's *Mingus Ah Um*, Ornette Coleman's *The Shape of Jazz to Come*, the Dave Brubeck Quartet's *Time Out*, and Miles Davis's *Kind of Blue*, which remains the best-selling jazz album of all time.

By the way, Miles Davis released two other albums in 1959 and played on a Cannonball Adderley album and toured. It was the year Miles Davis didn't get to go to the bathroom or make a personal phone call. No wonder he always looked so angry.

It is worth noting that 1959 also saw the release of the best-selling jazz single of all time, *Take Five* by the Dave Brubeck Quartet, which was the first jazz single to sell more than one million copies. And that's just a drop in the bucket that is 1959 jazz. Sonny Rollins, Horace Silver, John Coltrane, Chet Baker, Thelonious Monk, and more released strong albums in 1959. Damn, what a year. What could be better? Dischord Records, 1981? Hmmm.

Chicago and New York

*L*et's back it up a bit. As I mentioned earlier, around 1917, when the first wave of jazz in New Orleans gave way to the big bands, a lot of musicians, seeking to leave behind the racist bullshit of the South, moved to Kansas City. But some of them kept moving, all the way up to Chicago. For a while, Chicago was considered the Jazz Capital of the World.

You may find this hard to believe, but in the early 1920s jazz was rare in New York City. People objected to it on moral grounds. On moral grounds. In New York City! But then something even more unbelievable happened in New York City: they elected a cool mayor.

Jimmy Walker wanted to be a musician and even wrote a hit song in 1906, so he was sympathetic to jazz. In fact, he was a fan. Eventually, he gave up music to get a "real job," just like your mom is always telling you to do, and got into politics. And in 1926, Jimmy Walker became mayor of New York.

He turned a blind eye to alcohol, which was illegal at the time under the 18th Amendment, and speakeasies proliferated, with jazz providing the seedy background music. Meanwhile, jazz cooled off in Chicago and the musicians started moving to New York to party with the cool mayor's blessing. Of course, the cool mayor didn't last. Allowing all those illegal jazz clubs to operate meant that a lot of palms got greased with cash, including the cool mayor's palm. Awash in scandals, he resigned from office in 1932, just before Governor Franklin D. Roosevelt could have him removed, like the evil dean in an '80s movie. But by then, jazz was an unstoppable force in New York. And when Prohibition ended the next year, New York got grittier and smellier, paving the way for Agnostic Front, yo.

By the 1950s, New York City was the Jazz Capital of the World, also known as the Fourth Cradle of Jazz. Jazz was made for the city. New York had the infrastructure for jazz, including many of the key record labels, the best recording studios in the world, and a network of clubs. In short, New York was alright if you liked saxophones.

The most famous jazz club in the world, Birdland, opened in New York in 1949. Of course, it was named after the king of bebop, Charlie Parker. Ironically—that word again—by 1954 Charlie Parker was banned from the club that bore his nickname, due to his drug habits and unpredictability.

It was in clubs like Birdland where jazz played to a select crowd, where musicians honed their chops, and new styles like cool jazz evolved. (Compare this to punk's New York incubator, CBGB, or the Mabuhay Gardens in San Francisco.) Sadly, two people were murdered inside Birdland—within a matter of weeks—in the most important jazz year, 1959.

West Coast Jazz and Miles Davis Gets Pissed

New York City had the powerhouse jazz labels Blue Note, Prestige, and Columbia. Los Angeles had Pacific Jazz Records.

Pacific Jazz Records was founded in 1952 by two white guys, record producer Richard Bock and drummer Roy Harte, and specialized in cool jazz coming from the West Coast. Unlike most of the other jazz labels in the world, almost all their artists were white guys, including Gerry Mulligan, Don Ellis, and Jim Hall. There is no evidence that this was a racist thing. Pacific Jazz Records just signed artists they knew and had working relationships with, and they were almost all white guys. Miles Davis hated this.

If you read the Miles Davis autobiography, he brings up race every three or four pages. He turns everything into a race issue. And in most cases, he was probably right. So, when a bunch of white guys in California started playing music that was primarily invented by and played for Black people, Miles Davis cried foul. Well, what he actually said was probably far more colorful than "foul." In fact, if you read *Miles: The Autobiography*, you'll notice that every other word is "motherfucker." (Seriously. Maybe he got paid by the word. Whenever Miles Davis comes up in a jazz anecdote, you can be sure that he's going to be pissed off and profanity will be used. He makes *Damaged*-era Henry Rollins seem approachable.)

One of the things that Miles Davis objected to was that the term "West Coast jazz" was starting to be used interchangeably with "cool jazz." Davis was born in Illinois, virtually invented cool jazz, and recorded his major works in Kansas City and New York. Can you blame him for being a little mad?

But the main thorn in Miles Davis's side was Pacific Jazz Records' golden boy, a great-looking white Okie named Chet Baker. Baker was unbelievably handsome. Really. Ethan Hawke played Chet Baker in a movie, and he *almost* wasn't good looking enough to pull it off. Some have called Baker the James Dean of jazz. There is a good resemblance, and they were both cool, cool, cool. It's even been said that James Dean bought the Porsche that he ultimately died in because he had seen Chet Baker driving one. (You can bet your neck tattoo that Mike Ness has studied the Chet Baker charisma.)

Like Davis, Chet Baker played the trumpet. And he played it a little too much like Miles Davis for Miles Davis's taste. Further infuriating Davis was the fact that Pacific Jazz titles were being embraced by white America's cocktail-party people. And Baker was quite popular with young girls for a time, thanks in part to a friendship and working relationship he had with photographer William Claxton, who took stunning black-and-white photos of Baker and got them printed in teen magazines. For a blip, jazz had a bona fide mainstream heartthrob.

But Chet Baker also had bona fide talent. His music transports me. It is at once sad and romantic and has some elusive quality that brings me back again and again. You know, like Joy Division!

Hard Bop, Moanin', Skins, Brains & Guts

A reaction to the smoother sounds of cool jazz and West Coast jazz came in the mid-1950s with a jazz subgenre known as hard bop. Hard bop was a slight return to the busy music of bebop, but it also borrowed from then-popular rhythm and blues, traditional blues, and gospel. Jazz writer James Lincoln Collier expounded that hard bop was an attempt to make jazz Black again.

Saxophone and piano are key instruments in hard bop, which came largely from New York City and the emerging Detroit jazz scene. It is bustling, big-city music that you can feel in your bones. Some of the musicians associated with this strutting style are drummer Art Blakey, saxophone player Cannonball Adderley, bassist Charles Mingus, saxophone player John Coltrane, trumpet player Lee Morgan, and Miles Davis.

You may be surprised to find Miles Davis spearheading a subgenre that was designed to wipe out cool jazz, which he basically invented. If this surprises you, you don't know Miles Davis at all. Davis had a tendency to fire his band every two years or so and start over with a new group of people, just to keep things fresh and interesting. And about every five years, he'd change direction and pioneer a new subgenre of music. He didn't want to tread water; he wanted to move forward. You can say the same about Black Flag. You might not like all of their records, but they didn't stand still. For the record, I like all of the Black Flag records except the one that came out in 2013 with cover art that looks like it was done by 10-year-old Eric Cartman from South Park.

If I had to play you one album to demonstrate what hard bop sounds like, I would choose *Moanin'* by Art Blakey and the Jazz Messengers, released by the exalted Blue Note Records in the heady year 1958. And if I had to play you one 7-inch to demonstrate what hardcore sounds like, I would play the first 7 Seconds record, *Skins, Brains & Guts*, released by the exalted Alternative Tentacles in the heady year 1982. I really would. With '50s jazz and '80s hardcore, you can't go wrong.

The Butthole Surfer of Jazz

Another jazz offshoot, called free jazz, emerged in the late 1950s. Free jazz musicians were the real punks of jazz. They broke off from hard bop because they thought the style was too constricting. Or as the UK punk band the Fits would say, "Too Many Rules." In comparison to hard bop, free jazz records sound like a massive freak-out of improv playing. The Top Dog of Free Jazz is saxophone player Ornette Coleman, who released an album in 1960 called *Free Jazz: A Collective Improvisation*. It was his sixth album, so he'd been pioneering this odd style for a few years before it even had a name.

His 1959 album, *The Shape of Jazz to Come*, is a major mindfuck and my favorite. A self-taught player, Coleman crammed in lots and lots of squeaky notes, like a Greg Ginn guitar solo. He was a controversial figure. Miles Davis said that anyone who played like that had to be "all screwed up inside." Some even called him a fraud. I call him the Butthole Surfer of Jazz.

Part of the reason for Coleman's original, controversial sound was his instrument, a cheap plastic saxophone that had a harsh tone. You can hear it on *The Shape of Jazz to Come*. He couldn't afford a brass one when he was starting out but eventually did upgrade. Too bad. I like the plastic sax records better.

There's a video on YouTube in which Lou Reed claims his favorite song of all time is "Lonely Woman," the first track from *The Shape of Jazz to Come*. Then he goes on to "sing" the bizarre opening sax riff. Look, if Lou Reed says something is his favorite song of all time, you can bet it's going to be strange.

Free jazz records are usually the ones that make people say, "I don't get this. It's just noise." Well, that's what they said about Discharge in 1980! Anyhow, free jazz found its followers and the style has continued to this day. You just might get kicked out of the squat for playing it.

Hard Bop Continues Until It Dies, Coltrane Rises Above, Jazz Gets Weird, Another Kevin Seconds Joke

*T*t occurs to me that I haven't made a Kevin Seconds joke in a while, so let's fix that. What is Kevin Seconds's blood type? Do you give up? Kevin Seconds's blood type is B POSITIVE! That's probably not true, as B positive is a fairly uncommon blood type, but now you have an excellent joke for the next time 7 Seconds plays your town. I'm sure he's never heard this one before, either.

But we were discussing hard bop, which continued until the mid-1960s, a solid 10-year run, which is about the same as the Clash and about half as long as the Ramones. Some good 1960s hard bop albums to check out include the Thelonious Monk Quartet's *Monk's Dream*, Sonny Rollins's *The Bridge*, and Lee Morgan's *The Sidewinder*.

On December 9, 1964, one of hard bop's giants, John Coltrane, who earned his stripes playing with Miles Davis before becoming a star in his own right, entered a New Jersey recording studio with his all-star band and recorded a masterpiece in a single session. The four long tracks were released in January 1965 as *A Love Supreme*, one of the most beautiful batches of songs ever recorded. But the album was not considered hard bop; it was something else. Some called it post-bop or spiritual jazz. Coltrane, with his fast mind, was exploring new territory. His music got stranger on each successive album, much like that of the Butthole Surfers. By the time he died in 1967, it seemed like he was about to break through with something original and outrageous.

And by the late 1960s, hard bop was, in the words of jazz historian Scott Yanow, "running out of gas." (Over nearly 50 years, Yanow has written about a dozen jazz books, more than 20,000 reviews, and liner notes for about 850 albums, making him something of the Tim Yohannan of jazz. But unlike Yohannan, Yanow never wrote a review that read, "This is fucking great! This is fucking great! This is fucking great! This is fucking great! This is fucking great! This is fucking great! This is fucking great! This is fucking great! This is fucking great! This is fucking great! This is fucking great!") Once again, an old style of jazz was being made to sound outdated by newer styles. In this case, it was the emergence of soul jazz (sometimes called funky jazz) and jazz fusion.

Soul jazz is fun, sleazy, and slinky, and it feels a little dirty. Not as dirty as a Meatmen album, but still pretty dirty for the time. One of the most savory ingredients in soul jazz is the electric organ, usually a Hammond, for that gospel feel. Soul jazz combos are usually rounded out by electric guitar, drums, saxophone, and sometimes rich vocals.

My favorite soul jazz album is *Funky Skull* by bassist Melvin Jackson. This is serious baby-making music—hey, like the Meatmen! Some other soul jazz artists who light my fire are Bobby Timmons and Herbie Hancock, who both made the move from hard bop. Snobby jazz critics were not impressed by soul jazz, saying it was too simple and regressive. They wanted jazz to move forward into uncharted territories. That's where jazz fusion comes in, with the Most Interesting Man in Music, Miles Davis, leading the way. Jazz fusion combined the improvisation of jazz with bits of hard rock and funk. Enamored with Jimi Hendrix, Carlos Santana, and Sly and the Family Stone, Miles Davis began playing his trumpet through guitar pedals. Keyboards, electric guitar, and electric bass fleshed out the fusion sound. There was even talk of Davis working with Carlos Santana, but that never happened.

However, over three days in August 1969, Miles Davis and his hand-picked band of renegades recorded a milestone jazz fusion album. Not everyone was 100 percent behind it. Davis's long-time record producer, Teo Macero, sent a terse, worried letter to the executives at Columbia Records reading, "Miles just called and said he wants this album to be titled: *BITCHES BREW*. Please advise."

Nonetheless, the mind-expanding double album was released on March 30, 1970, as *Bitches Brew*. Honestly, this one took a little time to grow on me. The first song is more than 20 minutes. The second song is more than 27 minutes. By comparison, the first Circle Jerks album, *Group Sex*, is 14 songs in just over 15 minutes. So, from where I was coming from, this was quite an adjustment and a challenge to my attention span. Now, *Bitches Brew* is a favorite for long-night drives and low-light evenings at home. And it went on to be one of Davis's best-selling albums, the first of his albums to be certified gold.

The 1970s: Jazz Gets Even Weirder and Less Popular

By the 1970s, jazz was nearly unrecognizable from that first record by the Original Dixieland Jass Band. More than five decades had passed. But one thing remained unchanged: people were still running around saying, "Whooo—eee! That new music makes me feel like I'm gonna JASM!"

In fact, they were saying it more than ever, because in the 1970s jazz got sexy, weird, and unpredictable, the very same qualities you might seek in a Waffle House server. But sexy, weird, and unpredictable is not for everyone. For those with other tastes, the decade offered Fleetwood Mac, Captain and Tennille, Barry Manilow, and Valium.

The decade also offered the Clash, the Sex Pistols, the Buzzcocks, the Bags, the Weirdos, Devo, and the Pagans, who were all sexy, weird, and unpredictable in their own way, but right now, let's talk about jazz.

Seventies jazz started off right. Some of the best releases of 1970 included the aforementioned *Bitches Brew, Ptah, the El Daoud* by Alice Coltrane (widow of John Coltrane), two albums by Freddie Hubbard, and many more.

Alice Coltrane, one of the leaders of spiritual jazz, played piano and harp—an unusual instrument for jazz. Her records sound like they are from another dimension. A deeply dedicated Hindu, she took the name Turiyasangitananda and became a swami. Needless to say, her records are a lot to take in and can be off-putting if you are used to traditional verse/chorus/verse punk rock. Alice Coltrane is also associated with the free jazz movement.

Freddie Hubbard came out of the hard bop and soul jazz era, having played alongside John Coltrane, Sonny Rollins, Quincy Jones, and more. He put out quite a few great hard bop records, like *Hub-Tones* and *Ready for Freddie*, but in the 1970s, his style got more experimental, and he made albums like *The Black Angel*, *Red Clay*, and *Straight Life* that are, as you may have guessed, sexy, weird, and unpredictable. The one I find myself grabbing most often is *Straight Life*, which finds Hubbard playing what I like to call "detective jazz." That's not a real genre, but I love playing *Straight Life* late at night and driving around the city, pretending to be a grizzled cop who plays by his own rules, gobbling Tums by the handful and counting the days until retirement. There are a lot of Freddie Hubbard records and I have barely scratched the surface.

The decade rolled on with more albums by Alice Coltrane, Freddie Hubbard, Ornette Coleman, Pharoah Sanders, and others.

But by the early 1970s, Miles Davis noticed a couple of things. First, jazz records weren't selling like they used to. True, 1970's *Bitches Brew* was a commercial and creative triumph, but in general, sales weren't hot.

The other thing he noticed was that the audiences were getting older and whiter. Three or four decades earlier, a jazz club was the coolest place to be for young Black people. Some fans had been following Davis since his bebop years in Kansas City, but he wasn't getting many *new* fans.

Davis did acquire a few new fans by playing rock clubs and rock festivals, but the new fans were white kids, and, as previously stated, Miles Davis did not care for white people encroaching on jazz.

He decided he was going to make new music, targeted at young Black people. In rapid succession, he released a spate of fun, innovative, groovy albums, borrowing elements from hard rock and funk, including *On the Corner*, *Big Fun*, *Get Up with It*, and *Water Babies*. These are very listenable, high-quality albums—an excellent run for a middle-aged man, four decades and 20 albums into his music career. But the young Black people didn't notice.

Water Babies, released in 1976, was the last studio album Davis made in the 1970s. And while jazz continued through the 1980s and into the present day, the 1970s really were the last gasp, unless a Kenny G album is your idea of a good time. Creatively, it was a surprisingly strong decade for the music, even if the audience was much smaller.

The end of the 1970s is the end of my interest in jazz, but it is the beginning of punk. That makes this a good place to conclude Part One.

PART TWO:
NOTABLE ARTISTS AND
SELECT RECORDINGS

I remember my first four punk records: Dead Kennedys, Circle Jerks, Fear, and D.O.A. They provided an excellent foundation for my punk rock education. So to start your jazz education off right, here are just a handful of names and records worth your time and money. In the interest of not overloading your mind with too much information, I tried to stick to some of the biggest names, landmark titles, and key events. A lot of talented folks and amazing recordings didn't make the short list, but this is a pretty solid jazz starter pack.

Adderley, Cannonball

September 15, 1928–August 8, 1975

MAIN INSTRUMENT: Alto saxophone

TIME IN THE SCENE: 1955–1975

GENRES: Hard bop, soul jazz, jazz fusion

NOTABLE QUOTABLE: "You don't decide you're hip. It just happens that way."

SCENE CRED:

Julian Edwin Adderley was born into a musical family in Tampa, Florida. His father and brother both played the cornet. An attempt to start a band with his brother in Florida didn't pan out.

In the mid-1950s, Adderley was smart enough to know that if he wanted a career in music, he had to get out of Florida and up to New York City, the Fourth Cradle of Jazz. It was a good move, because in no time he hooked up with Miles Davis, who took him on the road for a year and a half in a six-piece group.

One of his bandmates in the sextet was the budding John Coltrane. This particular hand-picked Davis lineup was one of the most shit-fucking-hot lineups in the history of jazz. In punk rock terms, this is sort of like Henry Rollins being asked to join Black Flag right before *Damaged*.

Playing in one of Davis's bands was the equivalent of a Harvard education in jazz. Just about everyone who took the stage with Davis became an A-lister after leaving. But before Adderley struck out on his own, he, Coltrane, Davis, and a few other bad motherfuckers made the best-selling jazz album of all time, *Kind of Blue*, which gets mentioned a lot by jazz people because it is sort of like the *Rocket to Russia* of jazz. In other words, a must.

Adderley played on six other Miles Davis albums, including *Milestones*, and on albums by more than 20 other notable jazz artists, like Kenny Clarke and Oscar Peterson.

When Adderley left to form his own group, he called up his younger brother, Nat Adderley, and told him to bring his cornet. The brothers worked steadily in small combos until Cannonball died in 1975 after suffering a stroke. Little brother Nat became a headliner in his own right, finding a decent following in Europe.

Adderley got his nickname, Cannonball, as a bastardization of an earlier nickname, "Cannibal," which he earned through his voracious appetite.

WHAT TO CHECK OUT:
Presenting Cannonball Adderley (1955)

Somethin' Else (1958)

Baker, Chet

December 23, 1929–May 13, 1988

MAIN INSTRUMENT: Trumpet, vocals

TIME IN THE SCENE: 1949–1988

GENRE: Cool jazz, bebop

NOTABLE QUOTABLE: "I soon became aware that there wasn't enough time or opportunity to kiss all the girls in the world. The best thing is to stay cool—just be choosy and wait for the right opportunity."

SCENE CRED:

The Chet Baker story is perhaps the saddest story in jazz. And that's really saying something because jazz is full of sad, sad stories. How did one of the brightest stars in jazz, a talented man who looked like a Calvin Klein model, end up dead on an Amsterdam sidewalk in 1988?

It's ironic that jazz, a truly American art form, found a greater audience in Europe than in the States. Many American jazz artists made Europe their second home—or in some cases, their new home. These expatriates were thrilled to earn richer fame and fortune there.

And Black artists discovered the Continent was much more progressive than the U.S., where public schools were segregated until 1954, where interracial marriage was illegal until 1967, and where Martin Luther King Jr. was murdered in 1968.

Chet Baker was one of the biggest stars of the mostly white West Coast jazz movement. He, too, enjoyed the packed venues, the adulation, and the bigger paydays of Europe. But what he *really* liked was the drugs, which were stronger and easier to get than in the U.S. His first tour of Europe, in 1955, lasted eight months. Another lasted five years.

He also liked the fact that he didn't have to learn new material for the Europeans. While jazz kept moving forward with new sounds and new genres every few years, Baker was happy to stick with the cool-jazz tunes and occasional forays into bebop that he became known for in the 1950s. And the Europeans lapped it up for decades.

"In Europe they look upon jazz as art," Baker said. "In America it's a diversion. Somebody opens a restaurant and installs another band off to the side. People don't listen."

He must have thought he was in paradise: fame, respect, money, drugs. But Chet's European odyssey was not always easy.

Baker claims he started using heroin in 1957, but people who worked with him say he started years earlier, and history backs that up. On Baker's first tour of Europe, in 1955, his piano player and close friend Dick Twardzik died of a heroin overdose in Paris at the age of 24. Bandmates and friends say that both Baker and Twardzik were already experienced users by that time. The death had a profound impact on Baker, which drove him deeper and deeper into his own habit and haunted him for the rest of his life.

"Dick's overdose totally destroyed me. Destroyed me. Dick's parents felt it was my fault."

In an interview published in a 1964 issue of *DownBeat Magazine*, the *Maximum Rocknroll* of jazz publications, Baker misremembers the origin of his drug habit. "When I came home [from the 1955 tour], I started using drugs. I got busted several times, went to the federal hospital in Lexington [Kentucky]—then I got busted in New York and did four months on Rikers Island, and I decided to leave the United States for a while."

Back then, the place in Lexington was known as the Lexington Federal Medical Prison, and it was the first drug treatment prison in the U.S. Other jazz musicians who took the "Lexington Cure" include Sonny Rollins, Elvin Jones, Sonny Stitt, Lee Morgan, and many more. Ray Charles, Sammy Davis Jr., and writer William S. Burroughs were other famous inmates. Today it is known as FMC Lexington.

In July 1959, Baker, so bored with the U.S.A., returned to Europe alone. He made a home base in Italy, where he formed a pickup group with three local musicians. Thirteen months later, he was arrested in Lucca, Italy, accused of forging prescriptions and smuggling drugs. He spent nearly a year and a half in an Italian prison.

In 1962, he was arrested in West Germany and deported to Switzerland. Switzerland deported him to France. Later that year, Baker decided to move to England.

Months later he was arrested in England and tossed in jail for 40 days on drug charges. Upon his release, England deported him to France. He continued touring and scoring until he was arrested for a second time in West Germany and finally deported to the United States, arriving on March 3, 1964. He'd been in Europe for five years, playing music, getting into trouble, and getting fucked up. GG Allin must have been a little jealous of the guy. Back in the U.S., things didn't go much better. In the summer of 1966, drug dealers beat the shit out of Baker for an overdue bill. Accounts of the beating vary, with the number of thugs ranging from two to five. (Baker was inconsistent in his retellings and prone to exaggeration.) But the point is, Baker was seriously fucked up. He lost several teeth and, more tragically, his embouchure, the practiced connection between lips, teeth, facial muscles, tongue, and instrument that takes years to develop. Doctors said he'd never play again.

In a rare 1983 interview, Baker said, "My teeth were in bad shape anyway from all the drugs. I had so much pain that I decided to have them all pulled out. I got a denture, and when I tried to play again, I couldn't even get a sound out of the trumpet. So, I quit playing. I worked in a gas station, 16 hours a day for two years."

By 1968, the James Dean of jazz had to move back in with his mom and collect welfare.

Around 1971, Baker made a second attempt to reclaim his embouchure. It took him two painful years to rebuild. And somehow, he rebuilt it better than ever, developing more technical proficiency. The critics and the fans noticed.

His trumpet playing was the best of his career, but years of drug abuse had taken a toll on his once dreamy voice. It had become craggy and haggard, as had his appearance. He looked much older than his years. Baker, the former pinup boy with the horn, was being called "skeletal" and "ghoulish." His personal hygiene and sartorial choices dropped to new lows. Baker, who once wore stylish suits, took to sloppy jeans, ponchos, and filthy sandals. The sandals were functional at this point, as Baker preferred to inject heroin directly into his bloodstained and scabby feet—and sometimes, for the hell of it, his scrotum. He was shooting up 40 to 50 times a day.

By 1975, he was on permanent tour in Europe, where he felt more appreciated and where he stayed a step ahead of the IRS. Oh, yeah—Chet Baker didn't pay taxes.

His life was a never-ending succession of heroin, cocaine, morphine, opium, alcohol, and whatever else was around. All the while he was abusing Palfium 875, a European drug used to treat opioid addiction, popping 250 pills a day.

There was never going to be a happy ending to the Chet Baker story, and it was bound to end somewhere sooner or later. On May 13, 1988, Baker was found dead on a sidewalk in Amsterdam, just below his second-floor hotel room. Some say he fell; some say he jumped; some say he was pushed. He was 58 years old.

WHAT TO CHECK OUT:

Chet Baker Sings (1954)

Chet Baker Quartet Plays Standards (1955)

Grey December (1957)

Smokin' with the Chet Baker Quintet (1966)

In Paris (1973)

Mr. B (1984)

Embraceable You (1995, recorded 1957)

Basie, Count

August 21, 1904–April 26, 1984

MAIN INSTRUMENT: Piano

TIME IN THE SCENE: 1924–1984

GENRE: Big band, swing

NOTABLE QUOTABLE: "If you play a tune and a person don't tap their feet, don't play the tune."

SCENE CRED:

Count Basie, born William James Basie in New Jersey and known as the Kid from Red Bank, was a prolific composer and big-band leader for more than 50 years, staying active and finding an audience long after big-band jazz was succeeded by younger artists playing newer styles. You've got to respect that sort of tenacity. A series of fortunate events turned him into one of the biggest stars in jazz.

Before finding fame as a bandleader, Basie toured as a piano player on the vaudeville circuit for a couple of years, beginning in 1925. In 1927, he found himself stranded in Kansas City when his tour was canceled. He stayed in Kansas City, the Second Cradle of Jazz, and played the bawdy KC circuit for years until, in 1935, he assumed leadership of a nonet, a nine-piece band. Nobody else wanted to do it.

Basie and the band he fell ass backwards into running were asked to play a local radio show on a lowly shortwave station. That night on air, the radio announcer gave Basie the classy moniker that stuck for the rest of his life: Count. It was an homage to jazz aristocrat Duke Ellington. A powerful jazz critic and record producer, John Hammond, happened to be listening.

Hammond tracked the band down and asked them to move to Chicago—the Third Cradle of Jazz—and record with him for the independent Vocalion Records, a leading jazz label. Hammond called the session "the only perfect, completely perfect recording session I've ever had anything to do with."

Shortly after, Vocalion was acquired by Columbia Records, making the Count a major-label artist by default. By 1938, jazz moved to New York—the Fourth Cradle of Jazz—and Basie followed it, finding his peak of fame there.

Count Basie's various lineups hatched many stars, including Lester Young, Ella Fitzgerald, and Billie Holiday. He also played with Frank Sinatra, Bing Crosby, Sammy Davis Jr., and Tony Bennett, who were already famous.

Basie was known for his sparse style. He played fewer notes and left space between them, foreshadowing the coming cool jazz sound. One of his band members was quoted as saying, "Count don't do nothin'. But it sure sounds good."

Basie kept playing right up to his death at the age of 79. Oh, and he was in the 1974 Mel Brooks film *Blazing Saddles*.

WHAT TO CHECK OUT:

The Count! (1952)

The Atomic Mr. Basie (1958)

Count Basie, Volume I—1936 and 1939: The Count and the President (1985)

Blakey, Art

October 11, 1919–October 16, 1990

MAIN INSTRUMENT: Drums

TIME IN THE SCENE: 1942–1990

GENRE: Bebop, hard bop

NOTABLE QUOTABLE: "The people know more about [jazz] in other countries than in America. America is the last country to know about anything because we're too fat, we have too much of everything, you understand? And we do not listen."

SCENE CRED:

One of the things you will notice about Art Blakey is that in every picture he looks either like he's having the time of his life or like he's had just about enough of your shit. Either bursting with laughter or bored and agitated at the same time, like he's considering whether or not to give you a slap. Blakey could be hard to figure out. Oh, and his drumming is great, too.

I recall listening to side two of the 1970 Black Sabbath album *Paranoid* when I was about 11 and being astounded by Bill Ward's drumming. I'd never heard anything like that and assumed Ward was the greatest drummer on Earth. About 30 years later I heard an Art Blakey recording from 1958 and went, "Oh."

Blakey was a huge influence on hard rock drumming, especially Cream, Led Zeppelin, and the mighty Black Sabbath.[3] He played heavy and technical, yet his playing served the song. Anyhow, I was sold right away.

Blakey was a complex guy. Opinionated and hardworking. He was brusque and had zero tolerance for bullshit. He could be mean. Actually, he was kind of a jerk. With the exception of his drumming, there isn't a lot to like about him. The details of his life can be a little murky, and he sometimes contradicted his own history.

He was born in Pittsburgh to a single mother, whose name has been disputed. She died shortly after his birth and the father was not around. Blakey ended up in the care of his late mother's friend Annie Parran and her husband, Henry Parran. It's unclear

---

3 You can find a 14-minute video on YouTube, titled "Art Blakey & Ginger Baker Drum Duo," of Blakey and Ginger Baker, the legendarily quarrelsome drummer of Cream, going head-to-head in a 1973 drum battle. They're both smoking cigarettes—and smoking their kits. At around the 7.5-minute mark, Blakey tosses the younger Baker a look that could kill. At the 10-minute mark, Baker takes a beer break! I'm surprised this video doesn't end in a fistfight.

how many years he lived with the Parrans, but by the time he was a young teenager, he was working in the steel mills of Pittsburgh in the day and in jazz clubs at night.

Blakey was a self-taught piano player, but, as one legend goes, he was forced at gunpoint by a club owner to switch over to drums in order to accommodate a more experienced player at the piano. Some have called the colorful origin story into question, including Blakey himself at times. And other times not.

By the early 1940s, Blakey found himself playing drums for the handsome and suave jazz singer Billy Eckstine, who was also from Pittsburgh. But in 1947 the band broke up and Blakey went to Africa.

This quote is attributed to Blakey on the back cover of the 1957 Jazz Messengers album *Ritual*: "After the Eckstine band broke up, we took a trip to Africa. I was supposed to stay there three months and I stayed two years because I wanted to live among the people and find out just how they lived and—about the drums especially."

But in a 1979 interview he said, "I didn't go to Africa to study drums—somebody wrote that. I went to Africa because there wasn't anything else for me to do. I couldn't get any gigs, and I had to work my way over on a boat. I went over there to study religion and philosophy. I didn't bother with the drums; I wasn't after that. I went over there to see what I could do about religion."

He further befuddled jazz fans and historians with this statement: "Jazz is known all over the world as an American musical art form and that's it. No America, no jazz. I've seen people try to connect it to other countries, for instance, to Africa, but it doesn't have a damn thing to do with Africa."

It is true that while he was in Africa he converted to Islam, taking the name Abdullah Ibn Buhaina, though he continued to perform and record as Art Blakey. (He quit Islam sometime in the early 1950s.) And two years can't be the right duration of the trip, as Blakey made recordings in the United States between 1947 and 1949. For example, in December 1947, Blakey and a group called Art Blakey's Messengers recorded for Blue Note Records in New York City. It was his first recording session.

In any case, the prestige of the Eckstine gig was the stepping stone to other paying jobs with the likes of bebop stars Charlie Parker, Dizzy Gillespie, Thelonious Monk, and Miles Davis. Bebop allowed Blakey to really hit the drums hard and fast. (Interestingly, Blakey alternated between the traditional jazz grip and the matched grip style common among rock drummers.)

But by 1954 he had solidified the Jazz Messengers, a dynamo group with piano player Horace Silver and trumpet player Clifford Brown, exploring a new sound. The critics called the new sound hard bop.

The Jazz Messengers was originally a collaboration between Blakey, Silver, and Brown, but the latter two left to form their own groups, and Blakey became the de facto leader, renaming the group Art Blakey and the Jazz Messengers. In 1958, they released *Moanin'*, Blakey's calling card album and an excellent example of hard bop. The instantly memorable title track was composed by the Jazz Messengers' 22-year-old piano player, Bobby Timmons.

Art Blakey and the Jazz Messengers continued in one form or another for about 35 years. Some of the people who passed through the group became stars on their own, including Freddie Hubbard, Lee Morgan, Wayne Shorter, and Chuck Mangione, who you may know from the cartoon *King of the Hill*.

In keeping with Blakey's long history of confusing the shit out of everyone around him, he was alternately a preachy non-drinker and a heavy-drinking Muslim. And sometimes he did heroin. It was said that he could use heroin casually and it didn't affect his professional life. It has also been said that he had a penchant for getting his players hooked on heroin so he could string them along with the promise of more drugs. He was a heavy smoker, too, and died of lung cancer just days after his 71st birthday. Blakey left behind a few questions for jazz fans to wrestle with, but he also left behind a lot of great music.

WHAT TO CHECK OUT:

A Night at Birdland (1954)

At the Cafe Bohemia (1955)

Moanin' (1958)

Just Coolin' (1959)

Brubeck, Dave

December 6, 1920–December 5, 2012

MAIN INSTRUMENT: Piano

TIME IN THE SCENE: 1933–2012

GENRE: Cool jazz, West Coast jazz, third stream

NOTABLE QUOTABLE: "The worst thing about the life of a jazz musician on the road is getting to the gig. Once you're there and playing, it's marvelous."

SCENE CRED:

Dave Brubeck, a genial, well-liked, white family man from California, was a star of West Coast jazz, the more accessible flavor of cool jazz, who sold lots of records and divided critics.

I like some Brubeck, but he isn't among my favorite artists because I am not much for piano jazz. But he remains one of the best-known and best-selling jazz artists of all time, won lots of awards, and spoke out against racism. Even Miles Davis didn't hate him.

The Library of Congress designated him a living legend. And at the Kennedy Center Honors in 2009, President Barack Obama said, "You can't understand America without understanding jazz, and you can't understand jazz without understanding Dave Brubeck." So, what the hell do I know?

Brubeck and his two brothers grew up on a cattle ranch in Concord, California, which he called "a great place to grow up." Gee whiz!

Brubeck's mother had studied piano in England and had aspired to be a classical concert pianist. But she ended up married with three boys on a cattle ranch in Concord. She taught the boys to play in the classical style and gave occasional music lessons to locals. Brubeck's brothers pursued music professionally, but he assumed he'd just stay on the ranch and help his father with the livestock.

In 1938, Brubeck enrolled in college to study veterinary medicine, but a perceptive professor said to him, "Brubeck, your mind's not here. It's across the lawn in the conservatory. Please go there. Stop wasting my time and yours." He switched his major to music.

His early exposure to classical music left a lasting impression on him. Even the earliest jazz, from the kind played in the early 1900s in New Orleans to the kind played in Kansas City in the mid-1920s, had some classical influences. This was not lost on Brubeck, who said, "Do you think Duke Ellington didn't listen to Debussy? Louis Armstrong loved opera. Did you know that? Name me a jazz pianist who wasn't influenced by European music!"

(Classical-influenced jazz has been called third stream, and even Miles Davis put out a few albums in the style, including the fan favorite *Sketches of Spain*. But Brubeck was better known for the middle-class cocktail-party sounds of West Coast jazz, which could be alternately sophisticated and raucous—by middle-class cocktail-party standards.)

In 1942, Brubeck enlisted in the army; he was not drafted, despite what some sources say. He was sent to Europe to serve under General George S. Patton. But before he had a chance to get shot at by Germans who were definitely just following orders, he played a Red Cross concert for the troops. The concert potentially saved his life, as his commanding officer caught the gig and said, "I don't want that boy to go to the front."

Brubeck and his hand-picked group spent the rest of the war entertaining their fellow servicemen. They were even sent into the Battle of the Bulge—twice.

"I had the first integrated army band in World War II," Brubeck said. "This old colonel . . . was a humanitarian. And he allowed me to have Blacks in my band. It was against principle. I tried to get into a Black band. And being white, they wouldn't let me. So, I was glad to do it in reverse and bring two Blacks into my band."

Brubeck's progressive politics and intolerance for racism date back to when he was a child, and his father took him to meet a Black man who had been enslaved. The man took off his shirt to show young Brubeck the whip scars on his back. The impact of the moment lasted a lifetime.

After the war, Brubeck returned to California and to college, where, under the G.I. Bill, he continued his study of music. It was during this time that he began incorporating the unusual time signatures that would come to define his work.

"There's a way of playing safe, there's a way of using tricks and there's the way I like to play, which is dangerously, where you're going to take a chance on making mistakes in order to create something you haven't created before."

And it was around this time that Brubeck met alto saxophone player Paul Desmond, who would go on to be very important to his career. They formed an octet, an eight-piece band.

In 1948, Coronet Records, a small jazz label, decided to take a chance on Brubeck's and Desmond's group, and they entered the studio for the first time.

But Coronet was unable to keep up with their bills from the record-pressing plant, the Circle Record Company, which was owned by brothers Max and Sol Weiss, some of the biggest sleazeballs in the history of the music industry. In 1949, in order to satisfy their debt, Coronet Records traded their vault of master tapes to the Weiss guys, who in turn started their own label, Fantasy Records, with the masters.[4] Brubeck then made more albums for Fantasy, which were selling about 200,000 units a year—very good figures for an independent jazz label. But Brubeck's apex was still a few years away.

In 1951, Brubeck and Desmond trimmed the band down and formed the Dave Brubeck Quartet. This era of the group found them playing the college circuit. Some of these campus gigs were recorded and put on vinyl. The 1954 album *Jazz Goes to College* is a compilation of live performances from three college dates.

The Dave Brubeck Quartet was a hit with the college crowd, but not with the administrations—because the new bass player, Gene Wright, was Black.

Brubeck recalled, "I wasn't allowed to play in some universities in the United States, and out of 25 concerts, 23 were canceled unless I would substitute my Black bass player for my old white bass player, which I wouldn't do. They wouldn't let us go on with Gene and I wouldn't go on without him. So, there was

---

4 By the 1960s, Fantasy Records' bread and butter was Creedence Clearwater Revival, who, according to singer and songwriter John Fogerty, sold more records in the U.S. in 1969 than the Beatles. Of course, Creedence Clearwater Revival released three stellar albums in 1969, a feat later matched by Black Flag in 1984, and you know how hard they worked. Fogerty fought with Fantasy for five decades over unpaid royalties and ownership of the songs he wrote. In 1994 the dispute reached the Supreme Court with the case of *Fogerty v. Fantasy, Inc.* To read Fogerty's 2015 memoir, *Fortunate Son: My Life, My Music*, is to conclude that CCR signed the worst recording contract ever. Triumphantly, in January 2023, John Fogerty took to Twitter to announce that he had finally secured ownership of his music. I mention all of this to justify that "biggest sleazeballs in the history of the music industry" comment.

a stalemate . . . in a gymnasium, a big basketball arena on a big campus. And the kids were starting to riot upstairs."

Under pressure from the governor to defuse the situation, the college president told the band they could perform if Wright stood toward the rear of the stage. It was a bullshit compromise. The band went on with Wright standing in the back. But after a song, Brubeck told Wright, "Your microphone is off, and I want you to use my announcement microphone so you gotta come in front of the band to play your solo."

Wright stepped forward, joining the rest of the group, and, as Brubeck stated, "The audience went crazy. We integrated the school that night."[5]

In 1960, the NAACP publicly thanked Brubeck for his "courageous stand against submitting your band to the pressures of immoral racial discrimination."

Jazz Goes to College went on to be a big record; I think it is his most lively album. But critics much preferred the emotional, rollicking Black jazz coming from New York over Brubeck's heavily classical, academic take on the genre. Furthermore, the critics—and many artists—balked when Brubeck was featured on the cover of the November 1954 issue of *Time*.

It was only the second time a jazz artist had graced the cover; the first was the beloved Louis Armstrong. Brubeck, believing that he'd made the cover only because he was white, was embarrassed by the whole affair. He told Duke Ellington, "It should have been you."

Brubeck's scene credibility took another blow in 1957, when he released *Dave Digs Disney*, a jazzy reworking of songs from

---

5 The full story can be found on davebrubeck.com.

Walt Disney movies. I have never heard this record and I hope I never will.

But in 1959, Brubeck, Desmond, Wright, and drummer Joe Morello recorded some good new material, largely based on those unusual time signatures they loved so much. The executives at their then label, Columbia Records—home of hip East Coast artists Miles Davis, Charles Mingus, Thelonious Monk, and more—liked the sound of the new material but were not convinced it would sell.

A deal was made. Columbia agreed to release the cutting-edge album that would be known as *Time Out* if the group would also release a more conventional album. The quartet agreed, and the same year that they released their esoteric masterpiece, which would be the first jazz album to sell a million copies, they also released an album that nobody remembers called *Gone with the Wind*.

The success of the *Time Out* album has been attributed to the catchy third track, "Take Five," written by Desmond. The song received copious radio play in the Midwest, and people clamored for the album. A year and a half after the album came out, Columbia did something unusual for jazz: they cut out half of the song and released a single with what was left of "Take Five" on the A-side. The single also sold more than a million copies.

The late 1950s through the mid-1960s were the commercial zenith of the Dave Brubeck Quartet. They followed up the massive *Time Out* with several more albums in their trademark recherché style before the four went their separate ways in 1967.

Brubeck continued playing music with various lineups for another 45 years. He died a day before his 92nd birthday—on the way to a doctor's appointment, accompanied by his son.

WHAT TO CHECK OUT:

Jazz at Oberlin (1953)

Jazz Goes to College (1954)

Time Out (1959)

Calloway, Cab

December 25, 1907–November 18, 1994

MAIN INSTRUMENT: Vocals, bandleader

TIME IN THE SCENE: 1927–1994

GENRE: Big band, swing

NOTABLE QUOTABLE: "My audience was my life. What I did and how I did it was all for my audience."

SCENE CRED:

Cab Calloway was a popular singer and bandleader of the swing era. And just maybe you remember him doing a little song called "Minnie the Moocher" in the 1980 film *The Blues Brothers*. Yeah, that cat.

He was also a linguist and a lexicographer. In 1934 he wrote and published *Cab Calloway's Hepster's Dictionary*, a collection of jive slang. Jive is a secret language developed by Black Americans, with its origins going back to the times of slavery, when it was often a good idea to speak in code. And just maybe you remember Barbara Billingsley speaking jive in the 1980 film *Airplane!*

Calloway's dictionary was very popular, going through several printings between 1938 and 1944. It was the first dictionary written by an African American. The New York Public Library decreed it their official reference book of jive slang. Here's some jive we hep cats still use today, with Calloway's definitions and examples:[6]

---

6 Versions of Calloway's dictionary can be found in several places online, including at this address: flashbak.com/cab-calloways-hepsters-dictionary-a-guide-to-the-language-of-jive-1938-378657

Beat (adj.): (1) tired, exhausted. Ex., "You look beat" or "I feel beat." (2) lacking anything. Ex., "I am beat for my cash", "I am beat to my socks" (lacking everything).

Blow the top (v.): to be overcome with emotion (delight). Ex., "You'll blow your top when you hear this one."

Cop (v.): to get, to obtain.

Corny (adj.): old-fashioned, stale.

Gravy (n.): profits.

Kopasetic (adj.): absolutely okay, the tops.

Latch on (v.): grab, take hold, get wise to.

Lock up: to acquire something exclusively. Ex., "He's got that chick locked up"; "I'm gonna lock up that deal."

Sad (adj.): very bad. Ex., "That was the saddest meal I ever collared."

Salty (adj.): angry, ill-tempered.

Sharp (adj.): neat, smart, tricky. Ex., "That hat is sharp as a tack."

Square (n.): an unhep person.

Take it slow (v.): be careful.

And of course, there is some jive slang that has gone the way of Darby Crash, like "**Battle** (n.): a very homely girl, a crone."

But let's talk about his life and music. Calloway was born in Rochester, New York, but the family moved to Baltimore when he was 11. Baltimore is where young Cab discovered his lifelong love of music. He learned to play the drums and started taking singing lessons at 14. When he was still in high school, he joined his first band, Johnny Jones and His Arabian Tent Orchestra.

But that didn't last long, because upon finishing high school, he moved up to Chicago to attend college.

At Crane College, now known as Malcolm X College, Calloway began studying law. He also began playing basketball and performing in nightclubs as a singer.

By then, Chicago was the center of jazz, the so-called Third Cradle. Working the Chicago club circuit brought young Calloway into close contact with music royalty. At the Sunset Café, one of the most famous musicians in the world, Louis Armstrong, schooled him in scat singing, the nonsensical, improvised vocalization style of the era (later embraced by David Lee Roth). It would turn out to be the most valuable lesson of his life.

Basketball, law, or jazz? Calloway showed promise in all three areas and was even offered a position playing for the Harlem Globetrotters. Finding himself at a three-way crossroads, Calloway did some deep soul-searching.

Of course, he chose jazz. He formed his own bands and spent another year working the Chicago clubs. But by 1929, jazz started moving to New York City and Calloway followed.

Calloway's band, the Alabamians, got a coveted gig at the famed Cotton Club—but it was not a success. Their style of music was already outdated in New York—and what was the deal with that name? So, it was back to the practice space.

But a big break came when the Cotton Club called them back. Duke Ellington's band had to cancel a gig, and they were hired as a substitute with the boring new moniker Cab Calloway and His Orchestra. This time the crowd went wild. The group's style was updated, and Calloway was a visual and aural delight—white tux, wild hair, and smooth moves. The club owner took notice and hired the band on the spot as Ellington's replacement, launching a 65-year career that would take Calloway to unprecedented heights for a Black artist.

The group continued playing around New York City as Cab Calloway and His Orchestra and Cab Calloway's Cotton Club Orchestra. Their next huge break came in 1931, when Calloway and his manager, Irving Mills, wrote a catchy new tune called "Minnie the Moocher." A happy accident made the song even better.

While performing a radio broadcast, Calloway forgot the words to his own hit song and had to fall back on the scat-singing lesson he'd had years earlier at the feet of Louis Armstrong in Chicago.

"In the middle of a verse . . . the damned lyrics went right out of my head," he said. "I had to fill the space, so I just started to scat sing the first thing that came into my mind . . . Hi-de-hi-de-hi-de-ho."

The band echoed, "Hi-de-hi-de-hi-de-ho." And it went on like that! People loved the call-and-response gibberish. It went straight into the act and stayed there for decades. GABBA GABBA HEY!

While the iron was hot and the band was on fire, a record was made. "Minnie the Moocher" became the first record by a Black artist to sell more than a million copies. And Calloway became the first Black person to have a nationally syndicated radio show, broadcasted live from the Cotton Club. It was the Great Depression. Calloway was 23 years old and making $50,000 a year—or about $1 million a year in today's economy. He was one of the wealthiest performers of the time.

Calloway and his band went on tour, playing all over the United States. They were one of the first Black acts to reach Europe. They also conquered the Caribbean, Cuba, and South America. (To put this in a punk rock perspective, Minor Threat never toured outside of the U.S. and Canada, and they were fucking great.)

As one of the biggest names in music, Calloway was able to attract other big names to his band, including trumpet player Dizzy Gillespie and saxophone player Ben Webster. But the wild ride didn't last forever. After World War II, big bands fell out of vogue and smaller combos thrived. In 1947 Calloway cut his group down to a sextet and kept working, albeit to lesser rewards. And like so many of the greats, he kept doing what he loved—the only life he knew—until his death at age 86.

There are a lot of Cab Calloway "greatest hits"–type releases of varying shades of legitimacy on the market, and they all have the same stuff, sort of like Septic Death.

WHAT TO CHECK OUT:
Hep Cats & Cool Jive (2005; recordings from 1934 to 1953)

Coleman, Ornette

March 9, 1930–June 11, 2015

MAIN INSTRUMENT: Saxophone

TIME IN THE SCENE: 1949–2015

GENRE: Free jazz, avant-garde jazz, jazz fusion

NOTABLE QUOTABLE: "I wasn't so interested in being paid. I wanted to be heard. That's why I'm broke."

SCENE CRED:

One night my friend Kate told me that she had been in an all-female metal band called Thrash Queen that put out one of the worst records ever made. She refused to let me hear it and wouldn't even admit to owning a copy herself. Fortunately, everything is on the internet, including the Thrash Queen album. Holy shit, is it ever fucking bad. So bad I laughed. Then I started a Google search for more info and ran across what have remained my two favorite record reviews of all time!

EXHIBIT A: "To call these songs 'songs' is an insult to music itself."

EXHIBIT B: "Fuck this band."

Ornette Coleman, the bizarro saxophone player who played by his own rules and did so without a care for the critics, got a few interesting reviews, too. Here's one: "The only semblance of collectivity lies in the fact that these eight nihilists were collected together in one studio at one time with one common cause: to destroy the music that had given them birth."[7]

But at least that review concluded on a positive note: "Give them top marks for the attempt."

7 This is from a review of Coleman's album *Free Jazz* by *DownBeat* associate editor John Tynan.

And then there were the jokes: "A waiter drops a tray load of drinks, and a man says to his lady friend, 'Listen honey, Ornette's playing our song.'"[8]

The Top Man in Jazz, Miles Davis, was a Coleman hater at first, calling his music "unlistenable." Eventually, Davis came around to Coleman's unorthodox approach to music. But Davis's drummer, Max Roach, punched Coleman in the mouth after catching one of his shows in New York.

Coleman recalled the incident: "In New York, I'm telling you, guys literally would say, 'I'm going to kill you. You can't play that way.'"

British saxophone player and music critic Benny Green wrote, "By mastering the useful trick of playing the entire chromatic scale at any given moment, he has absolved himself from the charge of continuously wrong notes; like a stopped clock, Coleman is right at least twice a day."

What did Ornette Coleman, the Butthole Surfer of Jazz, do to piss off so many people? People like Miles Davis and Charles Mingus thought he was skipping the line, getting onstage and making albums before he'd practiced enough. But the thing is, Coleman did practice. And he could play conventionally. He just didn't want to.

"I could play and sound like Charlie Parker note-for-note, but I was only playing it from method. So, I tried to figure out where to go from there."

And in the liner notes of *Change of the Century*, he wrote, "The only thing that matters is whether you feel it or not."

---

8 According to Jo Livingstone, writing for newrepublic.com.

Coleman was born in Fort Worth, Texas. When he was a little boy, he asked his mother for an instrument, but she couldn't afford one. He made a shine box and went out shining shoes to finance his first instrument. He taught himself to play saxophone—from a book of music written for piano.

He joined a band in Fort Worth but was reportedly thrown out for improvising the national anthem, a good quarter of a century before Hendrix at Woodstock. He got an offer to play with a group in New Orleans, but that went even worse. After a show in Baton Rouge, he was beaten up and his saxophone was destroyed. "Some guys beat me up and threw my horn away, 'cause I had a beard then, and long hair like the Beatles." Of course, this was in 1949, a decade and a half before there were any Beatles.

Still in 1949, Coleman moved to Los Angeles, where he hoped to find like-minded musical adventurers. He did find them, most notably trumpet player Don Cherry, who would be his long-time partner in musical instigation. After a few years of jamming around California with Cherry and a few other oddballs, Coleman again needed a new horn. Lack of cash led him to purchase a plastic saxophone, made by Grafton. It was an alto sax, the only type Grafton manufactured, higher in pitch than the tenor he was accustomed to, and at first he hated the sound. It had a harsh, cheap quality that in time came to define his style, like Greg Ginn's preference for solid-state amplifiers.

Coleman, Cherry, and a handful of outcasts continued pushing their angular, atonal style, punctuated by shifting tempos and dead stops.

"It was when I found out I could make mistakes that I knew I was on to something."

Coleman and his crew got their big break when Lester Koenig at Contemporary Records, an independent label, saw something different and exciting in them. In 1958, Contemporary released the album *Something Else!!!!* to some controversy. Most people just didn't get it, but at least they weren't punching him in the face yet.

Something Else!!!! was recorded with a five-piece lineup of sax, trumpet, bass, drums, and piano—a conventional approach to jazz at the time. But by their next album, *Tomorrow Is the Question!* (1959), Coleman had decided to ditch the piano player.

This approach was not entirely unprecedented, but it was unusual. His thinking was that the piano provided too much structure. He wanted the music to breathe. The critics were kinder to this album and agreed losing the piano was the right step. This paved the way for his masterpiece, the album that really split the jazz scene in two, *The Shape of Jazz to Come*.

Now, by 1959, Miles Davis had released about 30 albums and been featured on several more. So, where does a 29-year-old newbie with a plastic saxophone get the audacity to call his third album *The Shape of Jazz to Come*? That would be like if Thrash Queen had called their album *Better Than Slayer, Bitch!* It turns out the title wasn't his idea. Astoundingly, Ornette Coleman, Don Cherry, and the gang found themselves signed to the mighty Atlantic Records just six months after their last album on the independent Contemporary Records.

Atlantic had a reputation for being artist-friendly and forward-thinking. Coleman's original name for the album was *Focus on Sanity*, but Atlantic's record producer suggested the more audacious title. It probably helped sell a few records, too.

Critics and fans were divided. To promote the album, Coleman and the group booked a two-week residency at the Five Spot, a prestigious New York club. The residency stretched to two and a half months as jazz fans, critics, and fellow musicians took the opportunity to see for themselves what all the fuss was about. (It was after one of these gigs when Max Roach punched him.)

But there were supporters, too, including conductor Leonard Bernstein. And like Miles Davis, bassist Charles Mingus eventually came around to the new sound, saying, "It's like organized disorganization or playing wrong right."

Forty-seven years later, NPR music critic Ashley Kahn summed things up thusly: "He was accused of arbitrarily breaking the rules of jazz when he was actually returning to a point when jazz had fewer rules." *The Shape of Jazz to Come* was one small step for Coleman and one giant leap for jazz. It freed things up. In fact, a few albums later, in 1961, he put out a record called *Free Jazz: A Collective Improvisation* What was meant to be just an album title soon became the name of a new branch of jazz.

This 37-minute album was recorded in a single take. The only break in action is to flip the album over. And that's not all: The album was recorded with two separate quartets. Coleman and his three partners play out of the left speaker while four other people play out of the right speaker. Before recording, the eight musicians only briefly discussed what they'd play. I bet the Butthole Surfers wish they'd thought of that.

The free jazz movement, of course, caused confusion among critics and fans. The funniest misunderstanding was when Coleman and his band ditched a crowded gig that was advertised as "a free jazz concert." The crowd was upset that there was a cover charge!

Just as people were getting used to all of the Coleman weirdness, he started pissing people off again by picking up the trumpet and violin without much—if any—practice. And like that, Miles Davis was mad at him again.

Coleman continued experimenting and flying his freak flag. Like Davis, he went electric in the 1970s and added guitars. His output slowed down considerably in the '80s and '90s. He had gone 13 years without a studio album by the time his last, *New Vocabulary*, came out in 2009.

Today Ornette Coleman doesn't seem as shocking and radical as he did in 1959, when *The Shape of Jazz to Come* went head-to-head with the more conventional *Kind of Blue*. In 2006 he was awarded an honorary doctor of music degree from the Berklee College of Music, and in 2007 he won a Pulitzer. Ornette Coleman died in New York City in 2015 at the age of 85.

In 2006, *New York Times* music critic Ben Ratliff had this to say: "The general message of Ornette's music is that it's for anybody."

WHAT TO CHECK OUT:

Something Else!!!! (1958)

Tomorrow Is the Question! (1959)

The Shape of Jazz to Come (1959)

Change of the Century (1960)

Free Jazz: A Collective Improvisation (1961)

At the Golden Circle Stockholm (1966)

Coltrane, Alice

August 27, 1937–January 12, 2007

MAIN INSTRUMENT: harp, piano, organ

TIME IN THE SCENE: 1962–2006

GENRE: spiritual jazz, avant-garde jazz, free jazz

NOTABLE QUOTABLE: "I came through the bebop era, and to me that was enough."

SCENE CRED:

When aging punk rockers such as myself get together socially, the conversation usually turns to the state of our hairlines and waistlines. And sometimes we talk about music. During one of these meetings of the minds, a friend mentioned that the Nebraskan punk band Power of the Spoken Word may be the ultimate outsider group, misfits among misfits, geeks with guitars. Their sole vinyl output, *The Language of a Dying Breed*, a little-known artifact, looks and sounds exactly like what it is: bizarre young men who read a lot of books, living in a culturally isolated place, playing their unique interpretation of punk. It's such an odd record that just calling it "punk" is a disservice. A lot of people hate it.

Alice Coltrane is kind of in the same boat. She didn't live in cultural isolation; she was married to John Coltrane and was intimately connected to jazz even before they met. But her music sounds like it comes from a yet-to-be-discovered planet. For starters, she played the harp, an instrument rarely found outside of classical music and Led Zeppelin albums. Like Power of the Spoken Word, she has a fan base in the form of a secret club that you may be happy to have stumbled upon. Alice Coltrane was never one of the A-listers of jazz, but her music is some of the most intriguing, even if you hate it.

She was born in Detroit in 1937 as Alice McLeod, and music and religion were always part of her life. Only the form of the music and religion would evolve over the years. She was the fifth of six children. Her half-brother was a jazz bassist. Her younger sister became a songwriter for Motown Records. Her mother was in the church choir. Like so many of the greats, she was introduced to music through gospel. When Alice was just nine, she became the organist at Mount Olive Baptist Church.

In 1959, at the age of 22, she moved to Paris to study classical music and jazz, her two primary interests. By 1960, she was working in a Parisian jazz club, playing organ between sets. At the club she met the American jazz singer Kenny Hagood and soon they married and had one child, a daughter named Michelle. But Hagood had a heroin problem and the marriage ended quickly.

A couple of years later, she moved back to Detroit, which had an active jazz scene at the time, and began playing the club circuit with various ensembles. It was at a Detroit jazz club that she met John Coltrane in 1963. John Coltrane's first marriage was about over at this point, and before his divorce was final, Alice and John were already serious. In fact, they had two kids together by then. The couple married in 1965, both deeply into music and deeply spiritual. They had a third child and John became the stepfather to Michelle.

The two Coltranes pursued separate musical careers until 1966, when John's pianist, McCoy Tyner, quit not long after the release of John's masterpiece, *A Love Supreme*, and Alice stepped in. In punk rock terms, this would be like Marky joining the Ramones right after *Rocket to Russia*. Both Alice and Marky missed playing on milestone albums by a matter of months, not that their subsequent work wasn't great, too. Alice and John played together until he died, about 19 months later, in the summer of 1967.

Alice took her husband's death hard. She was a 29-year-old widow with four young children. She developed insomnia. Her weight plummeted from 128 to just 95 pounds. She had hallucinations. Seeking comfort, she moved deeper into her music and spiritual life. Her quest led her to Hinduism and a trip to India, where she found enlightenment and adopted a new name, Turiyasangitananda, a Sanskrit word meaning "the Transcendental Lord's highest song of bliss."

And by 1968 she was leading her own group. Nearly a decade into a professional music career, she was, for the first time, a bandleader, playing piano, organ, and harp. Her brand of music was dubbed spiritual jazz. I'm about as spiritual as Marky Ramone's black Converse high-tops, but count me in.

It's widely speculated that John Coltrane was doing a lot of LSD in his last couple of years, and it's a safe bet Alice was doing it, too. Her solo music has a loose, light, mystical feel and seemingly no destination in mind. You really don't know where it will lead, but it's a nice trip. And the albums came fast, one after another. The first, *A Monastic Trio*, came out in 1968, but I think Alice Coltrane hit her zenith in 1971, the year she released two strong records, *Journey in Satchidananda* and *Universal Consciousness*. I think these two are a good way to get to know the music of Alice Coltrane.

Then, in 1978, after releasing a dozen albums in 10 years, she stepped away from music to devote herself to religion. She founded a spiritual community in California and spent the next decade studying religion and writing books before coming back in 1987 with a new album, *Divine Songs*. She sporadically released albums and played concerts until her death in 2007. As is true of many outré artists, her work is appreciated more now than in her lifetime.

WHAT TO CHECK OUT:

A Monastic Trio (1968)

Ptah, the El Daoud (1970)

Journey in Satchidananda (1971)

Universal Consciousness (1971)

Illuminations (1974)

Coltrane, John

September 23, 1926–July 17, 1967

MAIN INSTRUMENT: Saxophone, clarinet, flute

TIME IN THE SCENE: 1945–1967

GENRE: Hard bop, free jazz, avant-garde jazz

NOTABLE QUOTABLE: "Invest yourself in everything you do. There's fun in being serious."

SCENE CRED:

John Coltrane's recording career only lasted about 10 years, but he made a huge impact on music and is still celebrated today as one of jazz's most important figures.

In 1995, the United States Postal Service issued a John Coltrane stamp. In 1997, the Recording Academy of the United States gave him a posthumous GRAMMY Lifetime Achievement Award. In 2007, he was awarded a Pulitzer Prize Special Citation for his life's work in music. In 2009, Barack Obama hung a photograph of Coltrane in the White House. And the African Orthodox Church declared him a literal saint and opened a church in his name. Interesting cat, huh?

Coltrane was born in a small North Carolina town to a religious family in 1926. This is where he first heard the gospel and blues music that he would come to incorporate into his sound. Both his father and grandfather preached in the local church. By the time he was a teenager, the big thing was big band. And by his early adult years, beboppers Charlie Parker and Dizzy Gillespie were his idols. Coltrane started on clarinet but switched to saxophone after hearing Parker's sax player, Lester Young.

The Coltrane family moved to Philadelphia in 1943, a little after John graduated high school. He spent his days working in a sugar refinery, and at night, he played the clubs with whomever would let him play. Within a couple of years, he had his own group, a trio, with piano, guitar, and Coltrane on saxophone. On June 5, 1945, Coltrane saw his idol, Charlie Parker, play for the first time. As he later recalled, "It hit me right between the eyes."

Two months and one day later, Coltrane enlisted in the U.S. navy. It was August 6, 1945, the day the U.S. dropped the first atomic bomb on Hiroshima. Within days, Japan surrendered, and World War II was over. Nonetheless, Coltrane was sent to serve in Pearl Harbor. The fighting done, he fulfilled his naval commitment playing in the Melody Masters, a navy swing band. Coltrane, the only Black musician in the group, was never granted full membership. He was designated a "guest performer." When not playing music with the Melody Masters, Coltrane worked guard duty and kitchen duty, necessary but mundane labor.

Fortunately, Coltrane's lackluster navy career didn't last long. One year and two days after enlisting, August 8, 1946, he was officially discharged from the navy. With money in his pocket from the G.I. Bill, he returned to Philadelphia to study at the Granoff School of Music.

At Granoff he studied music theory for about three years until the G.I. Bill money ran out. And then it was back to the club circuit, where Coltrane worked as a hired sideman for the next nine years in bands of all types and sizes. Here was his real musical education. Of these club years, Coltrane said, "A wider area of listening opened up for me."

The silver lining of this time came in the autumn of 1949, when Coltrane joined trumpet wonder Dizzy Gillespie's touring band. But the dark cloud is that by 1951, like so many of his peers, Coltrane had developed a nasty heroin habit. It's too bad he didn't follow the lead of Gillespie, who wouldn't touch anything stronger than marijuana.

Somehow, despite the heavy heroin use, Coltrane practiced relentlessly. Sometimes he'd just work the saxophone keys for hours, clacking away without blowing a note. Other times he'd practice blowing a single note for hours until he fell asleep with the reed in his mouth. All of this time—more than a decade—he'd been playing clubs all over the country in various bands but had never been in a recording studio. But in the summer of 1955, he got a phone call that would change his life. Miles Davis wanted him.

Surprisingly, it took some coaxing for Coltrane to join up with the Dark Prince of Jazz. And he was modest about his early efforts in the group: "I am quite ashamed of those early records I made with Miles. Why he picked me, I don't know."

But Davis could spot talent. He was schooled by the great Charlie Parker, and just about everyone Davis invited into his inner circle would succeed as a solo artist. In his autobiography, Davis, using his favorite term of endearment, said of Coltrane, "I knew that this guy was a bad motherfucker."

In just four years, they made 15 fucking albums together, including some really great ones like *Milestones*, *Cookin' with the Miles Davis Quintet*, and the best-selling jazz album of all time, *Kind of Blue*. Was Coltrane being modest, or did he know he could soar higher? Whatever Coltrane was thinking, there is no doubt that those four years with Davis cemented his reputation as one of the leading motherfuckers in jazz. Coltrane referred to Davis often as "Teacher." He played busy and intense, in stark contrast to Davis's sparse, cool style. They went together like the Ramones and pizza.

Also in 1955, Coltrane married Juanita Grubbs, a Muslim, who would be a big influence on his spiritual life. Grubbs changed her name to Naima Coltrane. She had a five-year-old daughter when she met Coltrane. By 1956, the new family moved to where jazz was happening—New York City.

1955 had been a big year for Coltrane, but 1957 would be a personal, spiritual, and professional watershed. Miles Davis briefly fired Coltrane because his heroin use was out of control. During the storied nine-month layoff, Coltrane said, "I experienced, by the grace of God, a spiritual awakening, which was to lead me to a richer, fuller, more productive life." He quit heroin and alcohol—cold turkey. During this time, Coltrane studied the full array of major religions and came to the conclusion that they were all one. In the liner notes of his 1965 album, *Meditations*, he wrote, "I believe in all religions."

He also ramped up his rigorous practice regimen. And it was then that he developed the style jazz critic Ira Gitler called Coltrane's "sheets of sound," high-speed scale-based improv playing. Coltrane defined it thusly: "I start in the middle of a sentence and move both directions at once."

During this creative breakthrough, he spent months playing with the esteemed pianist Thelonious Monk, later saying, "I learned from him in every way—through the senses, theoretically, technically." To say that Monk was a more patient tutor than

Davis would be an understatement, and in the more relaxed partnership, Coltrane flourished. Davis noticed the personal and professional changes in Coltrane and summoned him back.

The reunion with Davis would last from January 1958 to April 1960. Coltrane was 33, and it was obvious that he was a star in his own right. He'd already recorded four solo albums for the respected Blue Note and Prestige labels. The teacher bid the bad motherfucker goodbye and even helped him find a booking agent and a lawyer.

In late 1959, not long after *Kind of Blue*, Coltrane was courted by Atlantic Records. Atlantic had a reputation for being good to artists, as the owners, Ahmet Ertegun and Herb Abramson, were music fans as well as businessmen. But just as with the 1955 phone call from Miles, Coltrane required some coaxing. Ertegun offered Coltrane a yearly salary of $7,000—about $73,000 in 2023 money—in addition to record royalties. Coltrane required more coaxing, so Ertegun sweetened the already-sweet deal by offering to buy Coltrane a new car. Coltrane chose a Lincoln Continental and signed the papers. It was a great deal for a young jazz man in 1959. He released four albums for Atlantic between 1960 and 1961.

Around the time he signed with Atlantic, Coltrane became an early supporter of the strange sounds of Ornette Coleman, the Butthole Surfer of Jazz, who so divided the jazz community with his saxophone freak-outs. Coltrane thought it might be time for him to get a little weird, too. He took up the soprano saxophone, in addition to his usual tenor saxophone, and hired the daring pianist McCoy Tyner, who had a similarly busy style to Coltrane's.

The creativity exploded. In late 1961, Coltrane jumped to Impulse! Records, which he thought would be a better home for his new sound. At Impulse!, Coltrane took off running, releasing 17 albums in about six years, each one odder than the one before.

By 1963, John and Naima Coltrane split up; the divorce was finalized in 1966. Naima said, "I could feel it was going to happen sooner or later, so I wasn't really surprised when John moved out of the house in the summer of 1963. He didn't offer any explanation. He just told me there were things he had to do, and he left only with his clothes and his horns."

The two remained in touch until his death. But as soon as the divorce was final, he married Alice McLeod, with whom he already had two sons, John Jr. and Ravi. Alice took the surname Coltrane, and the two would become spiritual and musical partners for the rest of their years.

It was during this era of musical, spiritual, and personal changes that Coltrane would create his masterpiece, *A Love Supreme*, which he called his tribute to God. The album is just four songs, recorded in a single session on December 9, 1964. But what a great four songs. Impulse! had it out the next month, January 1965.

It's by far Coltrane's best-selling and best-known album. *Rolling Stone* and NME have placed *A Love Supreme* in their top 500 albums of all time. The album has a permanent home in the National Museum of American History; the Smithsonian Institution has preserved it in their National Recording Registry. It's really one that everybody should have a copy of, like *Plastic Surgery Disasters* or *Zen Arcade*. The album starts with a beautiful gong and the next 33 minutes are heaven. I listen to it when I want to relax.

Not content with making one of the greatest albums ever, John Coltrane forged on. Even though he'd quit heroin and alcohol about eight years earlier, a lot of people think that in 1965 Coltrane started using LSD. The music sure got stranger. LSD might help explain Coltrane's 1966 album, *Ascension*. Perhaps in an homage to Ornette Coleman's 37-minute freak-out, *Free Jazz: A Collective Improvisation*, Coltrane, McCoy Tyner, and a handful of other risk takers went one minute further and recorded a 38-minute freak-out. It is a harsh, unconventional, atonal record. This was just six months after the release of the lush, accessible, universally adored *A Love Supreme*.

I had never heard anything like *Ascension*, and it took some time to grow on me—sort of like the second Die Kreuzen album, *October File*. *Ascension* has been called a turning point in jazz. Coltrane biographer Eric Nisenson wrote that *Ascension* was when Coltrane "finally became a full-fledged member of the free jazz avant-garde, with no turning back." Pianist and jazz writer George Russell stated that was "when Coltrane turned his back on the money." I listen to it when I don't want to relax.

Not everybody "got it," as in the case of a concert at Soldier Field in Chicago that saw most of the audience walking out confused. But the people who got it really got it, and jazz got far out and experimental. This truly was weird music that went on forever!

Coltrane released five more albums in his lifetime. Others, like *Expression* and *Om*, came out after his death. On July 17, 1967, Coltrane died of liver cancer, though some have speculated that the true cause was hepatitis, picked up a decade earlier when he was a heroin user. Either way, the death came as a shock to his friends, family, and fellow musicians. Miles Davis said, "I knew he hadn't looked too good. . . . But I didn't know he was that sick—or even sick at all."

By the age of 40, in a timespan of about 10 years, Coltrane had released about 25 solo albums, played on many more, and changed music forever. You have to wonder what his next step would have been.

After his death, a group of people in San Francisco, calling themselves the Yardbird Temple, began worshipping Coltrane as God Himself, using his music and lyrics in their services. In 1982 they aligned themselves with the African Orthodox Church, who told them that they could worship Coltrane but had to demote him from God to saint. The Yardbirds agreed to the Church's terms and conditions, and in September 1982, John Coltrane was officially canonized. And like that, the St. John Coltrane Church was open for business. I guess if you have to go to church, that's the coolest one you can pick.

WHAT TO CHECK OUT:

Coltrane (1957)

Blue Train (1958)

Soultrane (1958)

Giant Steps (1960)

My Favorite Things (1961)

Olé Coltrane (1961)

A Love Supreme (1965)

Ascension (1966)

New Thing at Newport (1966)

Expression (1967)

Om (1968)

Davis, Miles

May 26, 1926–September 28, 1991

MAIN INSTRUMENT: Trumpet

TIME IN THE SCENE: 1944–1991

GENRE: Bebop, cool jazz, third stream, modal jazz, hard bop, jazz fusion

NOTABLE QUOTABLE: "Motherfucker."

SCENE CRED:

While doing the fact-checking for this section, I tried to find a Miles Davis anecdote that I'd read somewhere. The gist of the anecdote is that a fellow musician approached Davis at a club, stuck out his hand for a handshake, and made some greeting. Davis took the other guy's hand, crushed it in his powerful grip, and growled, "I never liked you." My attempts to find the anecdote failed, but I did find a lengthy online discussion called "Was Miles Davis an asshole?"

Some have claimed that the famous Davis song "So What" was his standard retort to gushing fans. Others claim it was what he said to make actor Dennis Hopper shut the fuck up when he went into stoned, philosophical drivel mode. This was the man who, in later years, took to playing with his back to the audience. Fans were angered and confused. (Davis claims he played with his back to the audience so he could communicate better with his group—but he probably relished the anger and confusion too.)

You may have noticed that in almost every photograph of Miles Davis, he looks like he's about to kill someone. He said this was because the smiling face of beloved trumpet player Louis Armstrong made him sick. Davis didn't want to smile for the

Establishment; he wanted to scare the Establishment. He wanted to be the anti-Armstrong. One notable exception is the cover of the 1967 album, *Miles Smiles*. I think a lot of people bought that album because they couldn't believe it. Before we go any further, do yourself a favor and Google "Miles Davis and Kenny G." Terrifying, no?

So, was Miles Davis an asshole? I refuse to answer, because even though he's been dead since 1991, he still scares the shit out of me. If it is possible for you to separate the art from the artist, you may reap years of enjoyment from the vast and varied catalog of Miles Davis. And if not, there are lots of Kenny G albums. He seems nice.

And not to be too darn pedantic, but can we ever understand the Umwelt of Miles Davis? Let us try, motherfucker.

His life started out ordinary. It was even quite cushy, with educated, supportive, wealthy parents. Davis was born in Alton, Illinois, about 15 miles north of St. Louis, in 1926, roughly the time jazz moved from New Orleans to Kansas City. His father was a respected dentist and oral surgeon; his mother was a music teacher and violinist. Both parents were from Arkansas and the couple owned a profitable 200-acre hog farm there, providing additional income. He had an older sister and later a younger brother. When he was about one, the family moved to East St. Louis.

In 1936, Davis received his first instrument, a violin. It was his mother's idea. A few years later, he got his first trumpet as a present for his 13th birthday. Some sources say the trumpet was a gift from his father. Others say it was from an uncle or a family friend. But more importantly, Davis's father arranged for trumpet lessons from a man named Elwood Buchanan, one of his dental patients.

Buchanan was a music teacher and the high school band director at Lincoln High School. Davis wasn't in high school yet, so his father arranged for private lessons with Buchanan. Davis called the teacher "the biggest influence on my life." Buchanan encouraged Davis to work on technique and to strive for clear, round notes in the middle register. He eschewed the currently popular vibrato style favored by Louis Armstrong. Young Davis soaked it up.

By 1941, Davis entered Lincoln High School and joined the marching band, where he says he was treated with disdain by white band members. Prior to this, he attended an all-Black school, so it's possible that Lincoln was the first place he encountered racism and that it seeded his lifelong derision for white America.

Later in life he stated, "I hate how white people always try to take credit for something after they discover it. Like it wasn't happening before they found out about it—which most times is always late, and they didn't have nothing to do with it happening. It's like, how did Columbus discover America when the Indians were already here? What kind of shit is that, but white people's shit?"

But when one white Lincoln High band member disparaged his skills, he used the opportunity to dig deeper into his practice, later recalling, "I went and got everything, every book I could get to learn about theory." A year later, still a high school student, he started getting professional gigs in East St. Louis with a group called the Blue Devils. By the time he was 16, he was the group's musical director, in charge of scheduling practice as well as hiring and firing musicians. (In the decades to come, Davis would become the most prolific hiring-and-firing guy in the history of music. In fact, he hired and fired more people than Kevin Seconds and Adam Sandler combined!)

Around this time, an opportunity opened for him to join a professional touring band. He asked his mother if he could quit school to join the band. Mother Davis was against the idea and the teenager didn't speak to her for weeks.

Miles Davis graduated from Lincoln in June 1944; a month later he would become a father—for the first of four times. The mother was Irene Cawthon. The baby girl was named Cheryl.

Around the time teenage Davis became a dad, the famed Billy Eckstine band rolled into town for a residency at a local club. Eckstine's legacy is obscure today, but in his time, the decade before rock and roll, the smooth and stylish singer was about the closest thing there was to a rock star. And his band was stacked with ace players like Art Blakey, Dizzy Gillespie, and the patron saint of bebop, Charlie Parker.

Fortunately for teenage Davis, Eckstine's trumpet player became ill. Davis was recruited as a substitute and spent two weeks learning on the job from the best jazz players on Earth. Elated from the experience, Davis knew he had to move to New York, where the music was heading. The folks, knowing they couldn't and shouldn't stop him, approved of the plan. His father even suggested applying to the laureled Julliard School of Music.

This is when Miles Davis's life in music picked up momentum at an incredible velocity; any chance of him ever having a conventional life quickly disappeared in the rearview mirror. So long, Squaresville.

He easily passed the Julliard audition and, leaving Irene and Cheryl behind, started classes in September 1944. But Davis didn't spend much time in the classroom. He had better teachers in the city's nightclubs, teachers like trombone player J.J. Johnson, piano player Thelonious Monk, and his trumpet idol, Charlie Parker. He jammed with them whenever he could and studied the New York scene.

In December 1944, Irene and baby Cheryl moved to New York and the young family found an apartment. Soon after, Charlie Parker moved in, the jazz equivalent of letting Johnny Thunders crash on your couch until he gets his shit together. Parker was deep into his heroin habit by this time; Davis still hadn't touched the stuff. Cheryl was five months old.

After three semesters at Julliard, Davis had had enough. He complained that Julliard was too focused on European music: "The shit they was talking about was too white for me."

With his father's approval, he quit school to become a full-time musician. Although he had his complaints and didn't attend too many classes, Davis later admitted that his experiences at Julliard did improve his technique and comprehension of music theory.

In November 1945, the 19-year-old Miles Davis—not even old enough to order a drink—replaced the 28-year-old jazz pioneer Dizzy Gillespie in the world-famous Charlie Parker band and entered a recording studio for the first time, cutting songs for the famed Savoy Records. The next few years with Parker were an avalanche of recording sessions and gigs. Around 1946, Davis started using cocaine and drinking more heavily. The life of a professional musician was impossible to balance with fatherhood and family life: "I was still so much into the music that I was even ignoring Irene."

By the time he was 22, Davis's high-profile association with Charlie Parker led to his own contract with Capitol Records and his own titles. With a nine-piece band, he recorded three times in 1949 and 1950, producing a few titles that didn't sell much but reached the right ears and became influential to working jazz musicians, particularly the emerging West Coast players, like Chet Baker. This is much like record producer Brian Eno's assessment of the Velvet Underground. Eno is widely quoted as saying, "The first Velvet Underground only sold 10,000 copies but everyone who bought it formed a band." And that's how we got Sonic Youth.

Some of the Capitol sessions remained in the vaults until 1957 when the label, moving to capitalize on Davis's growing popularity, released *Birth of the Cool*, with 11 of those songs. *Birth of the Cool* went a long way in building the Davis fan base and spreading his influence among musicians.

Davis and his group were attempting to use instruments in a way that would approximate the human voice. The music has the feel of a relaxed conversation with a mid-range tone. It was a new approach to music, different from the complicated, high-end noodling of the Charlie Parker band.

Davis quit playing with Parker. Some cite a pay dispute. Others say that he couldn't or wouldn't keep up with Parker's high-speed, high-end-frequency jazz attack. Davis says he wanted to concentrate on the new conversational style. Around this time, Davis was asked to join the world-famous Duke Ellington band, but the confident 22-year-old turned down the offer to do his own thing, stating that it was time for jazz to change.

Foreshadowing Fugazi by decades, change would be a constant in the Davis catalog for the rest of his life. Every couple of years, he'd clean house by firing the whole band and starting over with new players, whom he was not too arrogant to admit he could learn from. He gave an astonishing number of musicians their big break and then sent them on. And about every five years, Davis would change style so much that the new sound had to be given a name: cool jazz, modal jazz, third stream, hard bop, jazz fusion. Davis was the spearhead of all these genres.

"I have to change. It's like a curse," he explained.

It's telling that such a young person could be so self-actualized. By contrast, Charlie Parker never changed. And the new genres left Parker in the dust, playing to older crowds, becoming less and less relevant until he died broke and looking like shit.

Davis toured Europe as a headliner in 1949. Europe was a success, but back in the U.S. things weren't as rosy. Jazz was going through a rough patch. Gigs were harder to get. Davis fell behind on his rent and bills. Stress and depression, which were present throughout his life, drove him to heroin.

It's surprising it took so long for Davis to try the junk, as he had been playing and living with Charlie Parker for years. Nonetheless, 1949 was the beginning of heroin and what Davis called a "four-year horror show."

To subsidize his heroin habit, Miles Davis took up extra work, transcribing music for record labels and pimping. In a 1985 interview with *Spin*, Davis said, "I was a pimp. I had a lot of girls.

They didn't give *all* their money to me; they just said, 'Miles, take me out.'" He was still with Irene, daughter Cheryl, and the couple's second child, son Gregory.

The 1950s were a fruitful but tumultuous decade for Davis. He recorded constantly, producing some of his best-loved music. And he toured a lot. In the early part of the decade, he and drummer Philly Joe Jones invented a profitable way to tour. Davis and Jones would recruit local musicians in cities across the country and play long residencies at clubs. They played more and had to travel less. And they barely had to pay their backup players. They called this approach to touring "barnstorming." I wonder if Glenn Danzig has looked into doing this.

But the decade started off shaky. On September 15, 1950, Davis was arrested in Los Angeles for possession of heroin. Word of the bust spread through the industry, damaging Davis's reputation. A lot of clubs wouldn't book him. They didn't know if he would play well or even show up. Of this era, Davis said, "I lost my sense of discipline, lost my sense of control over my life, and started to drift."

Things were not looking good for the problem-plagued prodigy. A particularly cruel slap came in 1953, when the *DownBeat Magazine* reader's poll for best trumpet player was awarded to his younger rival, Chet Baker.

Something had to change. In December 1953, Davis returned to his parents' home in East St. Louis and asked for help quitting heroin. Of course, his supportive folks had his back. Over a period of just eight days, Davis quit a four-year habit, cold turkey. He then spent months in Detroit, living in a halfway house and playing low-key engagements to get his skills and his confidence back. Davis chose Detroit because at the time it was hard to find drugs there. Yes, Detroit!

In early 1954, he returned to New York to rebuild his professional reputation. It was said that his playing was better than ever. He found new players, including Sonny Rollins and Horace Silver, and went about making jazz history. His performance at the 1955 Newport Jazz Festival solidified him as the top cat in jazz. Later in 1955, he recruited John Coltrane and formed what was one of his best of many lineups, the so-called First Great Quintet.

Nineteen-fifty-five started off strong for Davis: clean of heroin, a kickass new band with John Coltrane, critical praise. What could go wrong? It's jazz, so you know something is going to go wrong, but what, motherfucker?

In October 1955, Davis had surgery to remove polyps from his larynx. The doctor warned him not to speak above a whisper until he was completely healed. But the cantankerous trumpet player got into a screaming match with a club owner and permanently ruined his voice, making him sound like a hobgoblin mulling over the appetizers at Chili's for the rest of his life. The historical record is not clear, but one can almost hear him saying, "I'll take the wacky jalapeño zingers, motherfucker," although he may never have said that. Or did he?

The 1950s rolled on. Rock and roll was new and stealing what little thunder jazz had left. What incentive was there for young people to listen to Charlie Parker when they could pick up "Maybellene" by Chuck Berry, the other Charles from Missouri? In 1956, at just 30 years old, Miles Davis considered retiring from music. He was offered a job at a record label. He was offered a teaching position at Harvard. But once again, he found himself at a crossroads, and once again, instead of choosing a life of normalcy and stability, he chose music. Thank goodness he went for the gas instead of the brakes, because the last half of the decade was studded with stellar Davis releases like *Walkin'*, *Bags' Groove*, *Milestones*, and, of course, *Kind of Blue*.

The band was familiar with some of the songs that would comprise the masterpiece album before entering the studio. But Davis presented three of the songs to the group just before the tapes rolled. It has been said that Davis scribbled notes for the session in a cab on the way to the studio. Davis and his elite players recorded side one on March 2, 1959, and side two on April 22, 1959. The popular legend is that the entire album was recorded in one take, but that's not true. The song "Flamenco Sketches" is the only track that was a one-take keeper. Still, it is an impressive, cohesive collection of songs. Astoundingly, Davis called *Kind of Blue* a "failed experiment" in his 1989 autobiography. But a few million fans would disagree with him, including me. *Kind of Blue* is a melancholy, soothing masterpiece. I like to listen to it on Sunday nights when I am winding down. If you only listen to one jazz album in your life, this is the one I'd suggest.

Eight days after the release of what would be the best-selling jazz album of all time, Miles Davis got the shit kicked out of him by cops in front of Birdland, the New York City jazz mecca. He'd just finished playing a set at the club and escorting a white female friend to a cab. He was having a smoke break when, as he tells it, "This white policeman comes up to me and tells me to move on. I said, 'Move on, for what? I'm working downstairs. That's my name up there, Miles Davis,' and I pointed to my name on the marquee all up in lights."

A crowd gathered. The officer told him he was under arrest. Witnesses say the cop hit Davis in the stomach with his nightstick without cause. Two cops held the growing crowd back while another cop, an off-duty detective, came up from behind and cracked Davis across the head with a nightstick.

Davis was arrested and charged with disorderly conduct and assault on a police officer. He was held overnight and received 10 stitches in his head. The incident made headlines and made the police look like total fucking wankers. Photos of Davis in a bloodstained white suit caused an uproar. Davis threatened to sue the city and the charges were dropped.

"If you're black, there is no justice. None," Davis wrote in his autobiography.

On a happier note, in 1959 Davis married his first of what would be three wives. But it wasn't Irene Cawthon, the mother of Cheryl and Gregory. Wife number one was Francis Taylor. That marriage, his longest, would last about nine years—pretty good for a professional musician.

After the success of *Kind of Blue*, the 1960s began with promise. John Coltrane left to do his own thing. Davis selected the young saxophonist Sonny Stitt to replace him, an excellent choice. CBS gave Davis his own TV special, *The Sound of Miles Davis*. It aired just three days after the release of *Sketches of Spain*, a favorite among fans and critics. In 1961, he won the first of what would be many GRAMMYs and headlined Carnegie Hall. There was no Miles Davis album in 1962, but he was interviewed for *Playboy* magazine, a badge of cool at the time. No doubt a lot of people bought that issue to read the articles.

Over the next couple of years, he released a few more albums. The pace seemed to be slowing down a little, but the quality of content was high. He updated his band to include the inventive keyboard player Herbie Hancock and took this red-hot lineup to Japan for three gigs.

Nineteen-sixty-five started a series of health problems that would nag Davis for the rest of his life. He was diagnosed with sickle cell anemia and was beginning to get arthritis. In April of that year, Davis, just 38 years old, had a hip operation. Doctors grafted bone from his shin into his decaying hip. The operation required a long period of recovery. After three months in a hospital bed, the bored, world-traveling jazz master just got up and left. The operation was a failure. Ten painful years later, he would have another operation for a plastic hip. He released just one album in 1965, *E.S.P.*, sort of a sleeper in the extensive Davis catalog, but a good record. Though he recorded in 1966, there was no new album; a liver infection kept him in the hospital for the first three months of the year.

Nineteen-sixty-seven saw a creative spark, with two new albums, *Miles Smiles* and *Sorcerer*, both of which I really like. But more importantly, in late 1967 Davis asked Herbie Hancock to switch from a traditional piano to an electric piano. In early 1968, Davis added electric guitar and electric bass. By then, Davis was on his second marriage. Wife number two, Betty, a cool lady whom Davis described as "the best wife I ever had," as though she were a car or a pair of shoes, played some Jimi Hendrix and Sly and the Family Stone for the inventive jazz man, and he dug it. Needless to say, there were some freaky Miles Davis albums in 1968: *Nefertiti*, *Miles in the Sky*, and *Filles de Kilimanjaro*.

In October 1969, while Miles Davis was driving around New York in his Ferrari with Marguerite Eskridge, a 24-year-old white woman who was definitely not any of his wives, three men opened fire on the couple, squeezing off five shots. Davis was grazed; Eskridge was unharmed. The Ferrari took most of the damage. While the assailants were never caught, Davis surmised that they were hitmen sent to kill him by Black concert promotors because he'd recently worked with some white promotors. Just another day in the life of Miles Davis.

In 1969 Davis and his producer Teo Macero crafted one of my favorites, *In a Silent Way*, a groovy but soothing record that is perfect for late nights. In a single session, Davis, Hancock, and some other badasses recorded nearly four hours of electric jazz, which Macero masterfully edited down to two long songs. Side one, the song "Shhh/Peaceful," is a bit longer than 18 minutes. Side two, the song "In a Silent Way/It's About That Time," is nearly 20 minutes. Conservative jazz critics weren't impressed, suggesting that Davis was selling out to reach a rock audience. At least the rock critics liked it. *Rolling Stone* critic Lester Bangs wrote that it was "the kind of album that gives you faith in the future of music. It is not rock and roll, but it's nothing stereotyped as jazz either." It sold better than anything he'd done since *Kind of Blue*, a decade earlier. The album peaked at position 134 in the *Billboard* charts, which is shitty for a rock album but phenomenal for a jazz album. But more importantly, it was a transition to his second-best-selling album and a watershed in music, *Bitches Brew*.

Over a period of three days in August 1969, the 43-year-old Davis and producer Macero entered the studio with a large band and lots of electric instruments to create something entirely new.

Some of the musicians had been playing live with Davis and they'd already worked out a few bits of music, but Davis encouraged them to improvise, improvisation being the essence of jazz. He said he wanted spontaneity, "not some prearranged shit." The band set up in a semi-circle with Davis in the middle, snapping his fingers to indicate tempo and giving visual cues. For three days they jammed. Macero had hours of tape to listen to and laboriously splice together. The finished product, a 94-minute double album, was stylistically unprecedented. The funky, rock-inspired, creepy, electric, weird-as-fuck music would need a new name: jazz fusion.

"When you're creating your own shit, man, even the sky ain't the limit."

Upon its release in March 1970, *Bitches Brew* predictably confused and irritated old-school jazz purists who wanted everything to stay the same forever, like the Hummel figurines in grandma's kitchen. And although it wasn't exactly rock, the rock press mostly liked it. Robert Christgau called *Bitches Brew* "good music that's very much like jazz and something like rock." Langdon Winner's review in *Rolling Stone* stated that the album " encourages soaring flights of imagination by anyone who listens."

Bitches Brew is the second apex of the Davis catalog. To date it has sold about one-sixth as many copies as *Kind of Blue*, but it's a monolith, the sort of seismic record that blows minds even today, like *Damaged* or *Generic Flipper*. The album reached 35 in the U.S. *Billboard* and breathed some life into the dying genre.

After *Bitches Brew*, Davis even gained a few young fans in the rock crowd. He played a series of concerts at Bill Graham's famed Fillmore Auditorium in San Francisco and the Fillmore East in

New York City with rock groups like Neil Young & Crazy Horse and the Steve Miller Band. But Davis was a newcomer to the rock scene and had to play for reduced fees. Audience reaction was mixed. And he wasn't always the scheduled headliner.

As he told it, "I remember one time—it might have been a couple times—at the Fillmore East in 1970, I was opening for this sorry-ass cat named Steve Miller. Steve Miller didn't have his shit going for him, so I'm pissed because I got to open for this non-playing motherfucker just because he had one or two sorry-ass records out. So, I would come late, and he would have to go on first and then [when] we got there we smoked the motherfucking place, everybody dug it."

In the March 23, 1970, issue of *Newsweek*, he's quoted as saying, "I don't play rock. Rock is a white word. And I don't like the word jazz. . . . We just play Black."

Just a month after the release of *Bitches Brew*, Davis kind of said, "Fuck it! Anarchy rules!" Like the mad scientist of jazz, he began rotating musicians and making people switch instruments—live onstage. On August 29, 1970, Miles Davis and his crew of musical pirates played the enormous Isle of Wight music festival with Jimi Hendrix, the Doors, the Who, Ten Years After, Procol Harum, Sly and the Family Stone, and more. Guinness World Records estimates that between 600,000 and 700,000 people were in attendance, more than at Woodstock; this was uncharted territory for a jazz ensemble. It would be the largest audience of his long career. Just before he went onstage, someone asked him what he'd be playing.

"Call it anything," he replied.

Davis and Jimi Hendrix admired each other and talked about collaborating, but less than a month after Isle of Wight, Hendrix was dead. Davis attended the funeral, the last he'd ever go to.

For a jazz musician, Davis did incredibly well for himself. By the 1970s, a lot of his peers had died penniless. Some were still slogging it out in nightclubs. Several, like Bud Powell and Thelonious Monk, suffered mental health issues. In 1971, Davis signed a fresh contract with his label, Columbia Records, for a $100,000 salary in addition to his record royalties. It wasn't Led Zeppelin money, but for a jazz player it was unheard of.

Davis was riding high—perhaps literally—when in October 1972 he crashed his Lamborghini in New York City. He shattered both ankles and had to cancel months of tour dates. He healed up from the accident and took off running with a new lineup. In March 1973, he was back at Carnegie Hall to record a live album. He thought it would be a good idea to audition two new players, live onstage, without telling anyone else in the band—while the tapes were rolling. The resulting live album, *Dark Magus*, is 101 minutes of pure chaos, rivaling the intensity of Chrome or Void. The middle-aged maestro still had a few tricks up his sleeve, and he seemed to be loving it.

More solid 1970s Davis albums followed. *On the Corner*, an attempt to attract young Black people to jazz, missed its target audience and was largely ignored. It sold poorly and was panned by critics. A *Guardian* article calls it "the most hated album in jazz." Even the guy who played saxophone on the album said, "I didn't think much of it." But today it is rightly heralded as a lost classic. It's a fun, funky record that sounds like it could have been the soundtrack to a *Fat Albert* cartoon. I play *On the Corner* a lot and recently gave someone a new pressing as a birthday present.

Get Up with It, released in 1974, sounds like a cross between '70s porno music and a horror movie soundtrack; one song is called "Rated X." It's a sleazy, slinky, dim-lights album that I love.

In late 1975, multiple health issues put Davis out of action. In a short period, he had a bleeding ulcer, arthritis, and pneumonia. In September of that year, he had his second hip operation. The music leading right up to then was some of his most interesting, even if it wasn't as commercially successful or critically acclaimed as *Bitches Brew*.

He considered himself done with music. But professional musicians generally don't know how to quit. The health issues and boredom led to depression, cocaine, and heavy drinking. He was also having lots of sex with lots of random women. At least he was between wives at the time. As he put it, "Sex and drugs took the place music had occupied in my life."

The break lasted six years and it was not good for him in any way. His nephew, Vince Wilburn, a musician, could see the decline. Wilburn played some of his music for Davis and asked him if he'd add some horn. And like that, Davis was out of retirement.

"Music is an addiction."

Fans were excited that Davis was back. But the post-hiatus Davis material is his weakest. Creatively, he'd spent his best ideas years earlier. And having not played in years, he'd lost his embouchure. It would take hard work to reclaim. But what else was the jazz legend going to do with the rest of his life? Shuffleboard?

Davis spent most of the decade recording, touring, and running a media victory lap. The 1981 album, *The Man with the*

Horn, sold well but was panned by critics. The 1982 album, *We Want Miles*, won a GRAMMY. The 1983 album, *Star People*, is inventive but not a Davis classic. On October 17, 1981, Davis was the musical host of *Saturday Night Live*, two weeks before Fear's infamous Halloween performance. On *The Dick Cavett Show*, he taught a young Nicholas Cage how to hold a trumpet. There was his cameo in the Bill Murray movie *Scrooged*. He played a pimp on an episode of *Miami Vice*. He did Letterman.

In June 1982, shortly after a stroke that left Davis's right side partially paralyzed, Bryant Gumbel interviewed him on *The Today Show*. Gumbel asked him what he looked for when choosing a new band member. Davis, slumped in a chair, wearing a white captain's hat, and clutching a cane in his gnarled right hand—looking very much like a William Faulkner villain—replied in his raspy, weathered voice, "Carriage, what he wears, the way he walks, the way he talks." It didn't seem like he was kidding.

He added horn to albums by Scritti Politti, Chaka Khan, Cameo, and Toto. Music writer Greg Tate wrote, "Like Picasso when he ran out of ideas, Miles has taken to enjoying poking a little fun at himself."

On Aug 25, 1991, the 65-year-old played his last concert at the Hollywood Bowl in Los Angeles. In early September, he was admitted to a hospital near his home in Santa Monica, California, with breathing problems associated with bronchial pneumonia. At the hospital, he got into a yelling match with doctors. He yelled so fucking much he gave himself a massive brain hemorrhage. After several days on life support, doctors pulled the plug.

Miles Davis spent almost his entire life doing whatever the fuck he wanted, which is punk as fuck. But his search-and-destroy approach to life did take a toll on his body, and it was disastrous for his personal relationships. This is a sadly common theme in music of all types. However, he left behind a staggering catalog of music—most of which is excellent—that people are still listening to decades later. I have no doubt that people will be listening to his work as long as there's a way to listen to music. Not *ordinary* fucking people, mind you. He wouldn't have wanted it that way.

WHAT TO CHECK OUT:

Birth of the Cool (1957)

Milestones (1958)

Kind of Blue (1959)

Sketches of Spain (1960)

Miles Smiles (1967)

In a Silent Way (1969)

Bitches Brew (1970)

On the Corner (1972)

Get Up with It (1974)

Dolphy, Eric

June 20, 1928–June 29, 1964

MAIN INSTRUMENT: Alto saxophone, flute, clarinet

TIME IN THE SCENE: 1949–1964

GENRE: Free jazz, avant-garde jazz, third stream

NOTABLE QUOTABLE: "When you hear music, after it's over, it's gone, in the air. You can never capture it again."

SCENE CRED:

Like John Coltrane, Eric Dolphy left the world way too early. At only 36 years old, just as his creative spark was getting really hot. A lot more Eric Dolphy releases—about seven times as many—came out after his death than during his lifetime. In fact, he died two months before the release of his career masterpiece, one of my top five jazz albums of all time, *Out to Lunch!*

Although Dolphy began working as a backup player in 1948 when he was just 20, his tenure as a bandleader and solo artist was short—about four years. But he squeezed in a lot during that short time.

Dolphy was born in Los Angeles to Panamanian immigrants. Like Miles Davis, Dolphy had parents who supported his interest in music. He began clarinet and saxophone lessons at six. His father built a soundproofed shed for him to practice in. While still in middle school, he won a two-year music scholarship from the University of California. Clearly, this young person had a bright future in music.

His professional music career started in 1949, about two years after he graduated high school. Drummer Roy Porter, a West Coast bebop pioneer, saw talent in Dolphy and asked him to join his group. Roy Porter's 17 Beboppers may not be a household name or even a very good name, but at the time they were revered in Los Angeles. Young Dolphy made eight recordings with Porter, playing saxophone, flute, and clarinet.

Dolphy served in the army from 1950 to 1953. For his last two years of service, he studied at U.S. Armed Forces School of Music in Virginia. Upon discharge, he returned to Los Angeles and played around town with various groups for about five years, until another drummer, Chico Hamilton, gave him a big break. He spent most of 1958 and 1959 touring with Hamilton, learning the business, and honing his chops. By the end of 1959, he did what almost every jazz artist of the era did: he moved to New York City. There, Dolphy reconnected with bassist Charles Mingus, whom he had met in California, and joined his popular group. Just a couple of months earlier, Mingus had released his calling-card album, *Mingus Ah Um*, so securing a spot in the group was a great way to hit the ground running in the big city.

Dolphy and Mingus had great respect and affection for each other and would continue working together until Dolphy's death in 1964. Mingus called Dolphy "a complete musician" and said, "He had mastered jazz. And he had mastered all the instruments he played. In fact, he knew more than was supposed to be possible to do on them."

Nineteen-sixty was a colossal year for Dolphy. In addition to playing with Mingus, he was in the studio 23 times that year. He recorded with Sammy Davis Jr. and nine other groups. Also in 1960, Dolphy formed his own group, got signed to a record label, and released his first solo album, *Outward Bound*. He recorded the material for three other solo albums in 1960, which would trickle out over the next couple of years. The Dolphy style is characterized by wide intervals—leaps between highs and lows—

which he said was an attempt to emulate the sounds of animals and the human voice.

With the exception of Dolphy's erratic, dizzying, fast solos, *Outward Bound* is a fairly traditional hard bop album. After that, Dolphy albums became less predictable. Perhaps that was because by 1960 Ornette Coleman, the Butthole Surfer of Jazz, was living in New York, too, and the young alien types were bound to meet each other. Coleman enlisted Dolphy to play on his radically experimental album, *Free Jazz: A Collective Improvisation*, the album that would become the name of an entire genre of jazz.

By 1961, Dolphy was playing and recording as a solo artist and gigging with Charles Mingus. Then he met John Coltrane. Coltrane was about a year into his solo career and spreading his wings when he invited Dolphy into his group. They recorded together 26 times that year. Those recordings are considered classics today, but at the time they were the subject of derision among snooty jazz purists. *DownBeat Magazine* called the Coltrane/Dolphy collaborations "anti-jazz."

Coltrane later said, "They made it appear that we didn't even know the first thing about music. . . . It hurt me to see [Dolphy] get hurt in this thing."

Dolphy spent most of his last couple of years on Earth recording and touring with Mingus. In 1963, he played on the album *Mingus Mingus Mingus Mingus Mingus*—a great one, for sure.

In early 1964, Dolphy made the jump to the jazz stalwart Blue Note Records and recorded his masterwork, *Out to Lunch!*, a record he would never hold in his hands.

Encouraging creativity, he told his players, "Everyone's a leader in this session."

After the session, he was off to tour Europe with the Charles Mingus Sextet. In Oslo, he confided in Mingus that he intended to stay in Europe after the tour. As many jazz artists discovered, Europe was more welcoming to their sound and the color of their skin. Dolphy explained, "I'm on my way to Europe to live for a while. Why? Because I can get more work there playing my own music, and because if you try to do anything different in [the U.S.], people put you down for it."

He also met a ballet dancer in Paris, Joyce Mordecai, and they were engaged to be married. Yup, everything was looking up for Eric Dolphy. But this being jazz, you know something terrible was about to happen. It should be noted at this point that Dolphy did not drink alcohol, use drugs, or smoke. He was straightedge before Ian MacKaye was even born, making me like him even more.

On June 27, 1964, Dolphy was scheduled to play the grand opening of a jazz club in Berlin. He arrived at the club appearing seriously ill yet still went on. But Dolphy could barely play. The show had to be stopped, and Dolphy was taken from the club to a hospital. Another version of this story has Dolphy being taken from a hotel room to a hospital. That is not the only discrepancy in the sad Eric Dolphy story.

Dolphy had diabetes and he didn't even know it. In one version of the story, he is taken to the hospital and given a shot of insulin, and he has a bad reaction. In another version, the doctors at the hospital assume that the jazz man must have overdosed on drugs and leave him to let things play out. Whichever the case may be, on June 29, 1964, Dolphy slipped into a diabetic coma and died.

WHAT TO CHECK OUT:

Outward Bound (1960)

Out There (1960)

Iron Man (1963)

Out to Lunch! (1964)

Ellington, Duke

April 29, 1899–May 24, 1974

MAIN INSTRUMENT: Piano

TIME IN THE SCENE: 1914–1974

GENRE: Big band, orchestral jazz

NOTABLE QUOTABLE: "What would you be without music?"

SCENE CRED:

By now just about everyone is familiar with the old saying, "Kevin Seconds has written more songs than Duke Ellington and Adam Sandler combined," but for once, this isn't about Kevin Seconds.

Depending on the source, Ellington is said to have written or co-written between 1,000 and 3,000 songs. And it is common knowledge that Adam Sandler has written "The Chanukah Song" and "The Thanksgiving Song." Ergo, Kevin Seconds has written—A LOT OF DAMN SONGS! Of course, they can't all be as good as "Clenched Fists, Black Eyes," but this should give you some frame of reference for the genius of Duke Ellington.

Here are some other Duke Ellington/Kevin Seconds factoids:[9]

- In 1966, President Lyndon B. Johnson awarded Duke Ellington the President's Gold Medal. (Kevin Seconds never even met President Johnson.)

- In 1969, President Richard M. Nixon honored Duke Ellington with the Medal of Freedom. (Kevin Seconds sang, "Kill, kill, Ronnie Reagan" in 1982.)

- Duke Ellington won 13 GRAMMYs. (Kevin Seconds knows Pushead.)

9 The Ellington factoids are from dukeellington.com.

- The United States Postal Service issued a stamp with Duke Ellington's likeness in 1986. (In 1986, I wrote Kevin Seconds a fan letter, but he never wrote back.)

But once again—and I can't say this enough—this isn't about Kevin Seconds.

Edward Kennedy Ellington was born in Washington, D.C., in 1899, the only child of totally righteous parents who, at an early age, instilled in their son a sense of dignity and pride that he would carry throughout his storied life. They let him know that there were certain people out there who would try to demean him and hold him back from success because of the color of his skin. For perspective, he was born just 34 years after the Civil War, when the country was still mending deep wounds. James and Daisy Ellington told young Edward to always carry himself with grace, to always speak clearly, and to always look his best, so that the narrow minds of the world could find no fault with him. What an excellent parenting strategy.

Edward took his parents' words to heart. His young friends noticed his suave manners, easy demeanor, and impeccable style; they began calling him "Duke."

Years later, when Ellington became a beloved artist, prolific composer, and world-traveling ambassador of jazz, he said, "My men and my race are the inspiration of my work. I try to catch the character and mood and feeling of my people."

But first he had a lot of work to do. Both of his parents played piano, and with music in the house, it was only natural that he started playing, too. Formal lessons began at age seven. But in the beginning, he felt that piano might not be his calling. He was more interested in baseball and claimed that a horseback-riding President Theodore Roosevelt used to watch his team practice. A bit later, young Ellington started playing hooky from piano lessons and sneaking off to seedy poolrooms. The raucous poolroom piano players ignited his interest in the instrument, and he began to practice more earnestly.

By the time he was 15, Ellington still didn't know how to read or write music. But that's when he composed his first song—in his head. He was working as a soda jerk at a place called the Poodle Dog Café when he mentally wrote "Poodle Dog Rag," sometimes credited as "Soda Fountain Rag," a jaunty little number that he eventually recorded. You can find it on the internet. This was the beginning of the voluminous Ellington catalog.

In the meanwhile, teenage Ellington's musical education continued. A high school teacher helped him write harmonies while Oliver Perry, a professional pianist and bandleader who took a shine to Ellington, coached him in attitude, technique, and sheet music.

At the age of 18, Ellington and a friend who played drums started their own group, the Duke's Serenaders. Acting as their own booking agent, Ellington found the group steady work in Washington, D.C., and Virginia. The group played private parties and fancy balls. They performed for Black audiences and white audiences—but not at the same time. It was still the era of segregation.

After about six years of gigging around the D.C. area, the drummer beat it for New York—that old chestnut again. He'd been offered the drum seat in the Wilbur Sweatman Orchestra. I know, I'd never heard of them either. And if my name was Wilbur Sweatman I wouldn't exactly advertise it. Anyhow, it was 1923. The flapper era. The beginning of the Harlem Renaissance. Jimmy Walker, the cool mayor of New York, was into jazz. A short time later Ellington made the move to the big city, too.

Ellington and his drummer buddy found themselves getting in on the ground floor of a new group, Elmer Snowden and his Black Sox Orchestra. (Apparently, all the bandleaders in New York had nerdy names at the time.) But pretty soon Elmer split, possibly to become an optometrist, and Ellington became the leader. Not wanting to be stuck with a dorkus band name, they renamed themselves the Washingtonians. Then they picked up a long-term engagement at the Kentucky Club and renamed themselves Duke Ellington and His Kentucky Club Orchestra. At last, his name was in lights. The group made eight records in 1924; Ellington received songwriting credit for three songs. And Kevin Seconds wouldn't be born for another 37 years.

In 1926, Ellington signed up with Cab Calloway's manager, Irving Mills, the guy who helped write "Minnie the Moocher." It was not a great deal for the 27-year-old Ellington. Mills took 45 percent of the earnings. But that's kind of how it was in the early, lawless days of the music industry. At least Mills had connections and could find opportunities for his artists. And when King Oliver and his Creole Jazz Band turned down a booking at the Cotton Club, the most famous jazz club in the world in 1927, Mills secured the gig for Ellington and his band. They renamed themselves again, the Cotton Club Orchestra.

The booking would be substantial: 1927 to 1931, onstage almost every night, playing for New York's wealthy, white society types. The group made several live recordings from the club. But perhaps the greatest benefit of playing the Cotton Club was the weekly live radio broadcast. In those days, there was little regulation of radio broadcasting, and the more powerful signals could be heard hundreds of miles away. This helped make Duke Ellington a household name, unlike Wilbur Sweatman.

During their four-year commitment, Ellington and the group did take a couple of short breaks from the Cotton Club to go to Hollywood and be in movies. The first film Ellington appeared in sounds OK. In *Black and Tan*, an RKO film released in 1929, Ellington plays a bandleader named Duke. I have not seen the film, but I'm sure he did not struggle with the role.

In Ellington's second film, he literally stars as himself. The 1930 film, *Check and Double Check*, is a befuddling commitment for a dignified Black man. The lead characters, comedy duo Amos 'n' Andy, are a couple of white actors in blackface. I have not seen this film, either, but it cannot be good.

All the while, Ellington was composing. Like a good boss, he knew each band member's strengths and weaknesses. He custom tailored songs to give each of his band members a chance to shine. His band appreciated this and repaid him with loyalty. Baritone saxophonist Harry Carney played with Ellington for 47 years. Another artist Ellington wrote specifically for was singer Adelaide Hall. The song "Creole Love Call" was the group's first hit and it made her a star.

And in 1931, Ellington hired Ivie Anderson, a woman with a huge smile and a huge voice. For her he penned "It Don't Mean a Thing (If It Ain't Got That Swing)," which everyone has probably heard at least once. (A later version was recorded with Ella Fitzgerald.) Anderson stayed with Ellington for more than a decade, touring the world, singing, and smiling.

Just before the release of "It Don't Mean a Thing (If It Ain't Got That Swing)," Ellington's engagement at the Cotton Club ended. The song was a hit everywhere, but the U.S. was struggling through the Great Depression. The group found more money and better conditions in Europe. In 1933, the Duke conquered England, Scotland, the Netherlands, and France with his style, humor, and infectious tunes. Then in 1934, the band toured the U.S. by private railcars, traveling in luxury and avoiding the dangerous realities of driving while Black through the American South. In 1935, the Cotton Club closed following a race riot, proving that the North could be just as shitty. It was the end of the Harlem Renaissance.

It wasn't an easy time for orchestral jazz bands. Swing, light-hearted dance music played by fellas like Benny Goodman, gained popularity, taking some audience away from Ellington and his more cerebral music. Somewhat bitterly, Ellington remarked, "Jazz is music, the swing is business." Ellington tightened his belt and reduced his band to nine, then eight, and finally six players.

"A problem is a chance for you to do your best."

The good news is that by 1937, Ellington had ditched his manager, Mills, and signed with the prestigious William Morris Agency, still in operation today as WME. Two years later, Ellington partnered with the talented Billy Strayhorn to write songs.

It was said that the two men had nearly identical styles of playing and composing. This is why jazz scholars today have difficulty determining which songs were written by Ellington, which were written by Strayhorn, and which were written together. People called Billy Strayhorn "the doppelganger." When Ellington couldn't make it to a practice—or sometimes a concert—Strayhorn could fill in seamlessly. Why didn't Strayhorn just go out and succeed on his own? In Ellington's own words, "There is nothing to keeping a band together. You simply have to have a gimmick, and the gimmick I use is to pay them money!"

Some of the better-known Ellington-Strayhorn collaborations include "Take the 'A' Train" and "Satin Doll." Both became jazz standards, covered again and again. You've probably heard them, even if you don't recognize the titles. I think "Take the 'A' Train" was used in an episode of *The Simpsons*.

And then the U.S. entered World War II. Musicians got drafted or enlisted. The musicians' strike of 1942, mentioned in Part One, meant there were virtually no records made in the U.S. for two years. A federal tax on live music clubs forced venues to hire smaller bands. Smaller groups with swoony crooners became the popular sound, and for all intents and purposes, big band was dead. But Ellington wasn't ready to quit.

"People do not retire. They are retired by others."

The post–World War II years found Ellington playing with smaller groups, mostly for financial reasons. And once again, he took the show abroad, to bigger paychecks and bigger audiences. In 1950 Ellington and his reduced band played 74 shows in Europe in 77 days, a feat even D.O.A. would be impressed by.

All this time, Ellington had been composing music with the limitations of the 78-rpm record (about three to five minutes per side, depending on the manufacturer) in mind. But by the end of the 1920s, he began writing longer songs, splitting them in two, and placing each half on a record side. Record buyers didn't much like having to get up and flip the record over just as it was getting to the good part, and I'm sure at least one of them compared this annoyance to coitus interruptus.

The 1931 song "Reminiscing in Tempo," which Ellington wrote in tribute to his mother, played across four 78 sides, necessitating a triple interruption of coitus. By that time, the casual listener would usually say, "Shit, let's just see what's in the fridge." The longer songs weren't popular live, either, with the audience's collective mind drifting from the concert to coitus and back again. A lot of people left these concerts feeling strangely unsatisfied.

But in 1948, Peter Carl Goldmark, a Hungarian-American engineer at CBS, invented the 33 1/3-rpm 12" LP. The new format meant that artists like Ellington could stretch their performance as long as 22 minutes per side, something this Hungarian-American writer has only heard about in locker rooms. But one thing we can all agree on is that the Angry Samoans really should have written a song called "Coitus Interruptus."

Nineteen-fifty-five found Duke Ellington without a recording contract. Jazz had changed so much since his halcyon days at the Cotton Club. The likes of Chet Baker, Miles Davis, and Dave Brubeck were foremost in the minds of what jazz fans were left. The Cotton Club was two or three jazz generations past. This would be like the Sex Pistols trying to compete with Minor Threat for relevance in 1981 Washington, D.C.

A lifesaver came in the form of a slot at the 1956 Newport Jazz Festival, the most lauded jazz festival in the world. At Newport, Ellington and his band turned in a firestorm performance, playing past the noise curfew, much to the distress of the concert promoters. The crowd loved it; the story made headlines around the world. Ellington made the cover of *Time*. But more importantly, tapes were rolling that enchanted evening, resulting in a record deal with Columbia and the live album *Ellington at Newport*. The late-career album remains the best-selling title in the Ellington catalog.

Finally, in 1961, Kevin Seconds was born and Ellington was without a record label again. But the Duke picked up session work with emerging artists who admired him, like Max Roach, John Coltrane, and Charles Mingus. He even played on records with his friendly rivals from the past, Louis Armstrong and

Count Basie. And he spent the rest of his life touring his ass off: Europe, Asia, Australia, Africa, the Middle East, South America, Central America, and more. Over a period of 50 years, Duke Ellington played more than 20,000 concerts. Compare this to fellow Washington, D.C., musicians S.O.A., who played just 9 concerts.

Like many of the greats, Ellington couldn't stop. On March 20, 1974, Ellington gave his last performance. And on May 24, 1974, he died from complications brought on by lung cancer and pneumonia, just 25 days after his 75th birthday. An estimated 12,000 people showed up at his funeral.

It was an ordinary death for an extraordinary person. Thank goodness Ellington never succumbed to the all-too-common occupational hazards of jazz: drug abuse, alcoholism, prison, poverty, and mental illness. Just a month after Ellington's death, Miles Davis honored him with the song "He Loved Him Madly." Later that year, Charles Mingus paid him tribute with "Duke Ellington's Sound of Love." Even Stevie Wonder eulogized him in 1976 with "Sir Duke," a song that was inescapable in my childhood.

Ellington left the world a ton of quality music and this timeless piece of wisdom: "If it sounds good, it *is* good."

WHAT TO CHECK OUT:

Ellington at Newport (1956)

Blues in Orbit (1960)

The Afro-Eurasian Eclipse (1971)

The Best of Duke Ellington (1980)

In the Uncommon Market (1986)

Fitzgerald, Ella

April 25, 1917–June 15, 1996

MAIN INSTRUMENT: Vocals

TIME IN THE SCENE: 1929–1991

GENRE: Swing, big band, bebop

NOTABLE QUOTABLE: "I sing like I feel."

SCENE CRED:

You can tell the Ella Fitzgerald story in numbers. A 62-year career. Thirteen GRAMMYs. More than 200 albums and more than 2,000 songs. Forty million records sold. And nearly 100 years after she started singing, people are still listening to her music and record labels are still finding unreleased material in the vaults. Few jazz artists have achieved this level of success. To put this in perspective, the first Roach Motel record sold 600 copies!

Fitzgerald was universally loved and respected by her peers. She was an A-list headliner and shared the spotlight with other giants of jazz, like Duke Ellington, Count Basie, Dizzy Gillespie, Benny Goodman, Nat King Cole, and the Tortellini Tornado himself, Frank Sinatra. She worked with just about everybody in the business except Kevin Seconds. Most of the world knows Fitzgerald by her title, the First Lady of Song. The nicest man in jazz, singer Mel Tormé, called her "the High Priestess of Song." Duke Ellington's songwriting partner, Billy Strayhorn, said, "Ella is the boss lady. That's all." To put this in perspective, a lot of people thought the singer of Roach Motel was kind of a jerk. But not me.

Fitzgerald was known for her perfect diction, clear tone, tasteful phrasing, and improvisational skills. To put this in perspective, Roach Motel was known for a song called "More Beer." Those were the only lyrics.

Aside from a bumpy adolescence and the health issues of her later years, Ella Fitzgerald had a pretty good life. She avoided the demons that plagued so many jazz artists: drugs, alcohol, and poverty. And she seemed to love her work.

"The only thing better than singing is more singing."

Ella Fitzgerald was born April 25, 1917, in Newport News, Virginia, to William and Temperance Fitzgerald, both of whom were biracial, with Black and white ancestry. Young Ella was a shy girl who called herself a tomboy. She carried her coyness all of her life. Like many performers, the only time she wasn't shy was on the stage when she let everything out. As she put it, "I know I'm no glamour girl, and it's not easy for me to get up in front of a crowd of people. It used to bother me a lot, but now I've got it figured out that God gave me this talent to use, so I just stand there and sing."

Her parents split up when she was a toddler. Temperance took Ella to live in Yonkers, New York, with her Portuguese immigrant boyfriend, Joseph Da Silva, and his daughter, Frances. The blended family was harmonious. Joseph was a ditch digger; Temperance was a laundress. As a teenager, Ella pitched in by picking up chores around the neighborhood. She obliviously found work with a local gambling ring, taking bets and delivering money. But more importantly, it was in Yonkers that she began dancing and singing with neighborhood kids, little knowing entertainment would become her livelihood.

Tragically, in 1932, Temperance was killed in a car crash. The 15-year-old Fitzgerald took the death hard. In April 1933, she moved to Harlem to live with Temperance's sister, Virginia. Not long after, Joseph died of a heart attack and Frances, just 10 years old, joined her half-sister and aunt in Harlem. The two quickly found out about the famed Apollo Theater, where stars were born, and watched in awe from the seats.

Besides the music at the Apollo, Fitzgerald's teenage life in Harlem was bleak. Though she was formerly an excellent student in Yonkers, her grades began to slip. She started skipping school and ran afoul of the authorities. Her only transgression was truancy, but the state sent her away to the Colored Orphan Asylum, which sounds like something from a dark Flannery O'Connor story. At the Colored Orphan Asylum, she was beaten by the staff before being transferred to the New York Training School for Girls, where she was beaten by their staff, too.

Then, Fitzgerald escaped from the institution. Later, when she became a professional entertainer, Fitzgerald would draw upon the memories of this crappy era to power her performance, like a method actor.

Fitzgerald's big break came on November 21, 1934. The 17-year-old signed up for amateur night at the Apollo Theater, where legends were made pretty much every week that decade. Really, you needed a program just to keep up with all of the new legends. (The programs cost 10 cents, but for that price you also got a cup of coffee, a slice of rhubarb pie, and a shoeshine.)

She signed up with the intent of doing a dance routine, but before her turn, a powerful dance trio brought down the house with their act. Fitzgerald recalled, "They were the dancingest sisters around."

Then came her turn. She walked onstage and froze. The audience murmured and some assholes even booed the scared teenager. Then she broke into a song called "Judy." The audience went nuts; they demanded an encore. Fitzgerald quickly thought of another song she knew, "The Object of My Affections," and again the audience responded with fervor. Technically, Ella Fitzgerald won the amateur contest. The prize was $25 and another chance to appear at the Apollo. But the judges thought her appearance was slovenly. They gave her the money but told her she wasn't invited back. But that was OK, because the teenager saw her future that night.

"Once up there, I felt the acceptance and love from my audience. I knew I wanted to sing before people the rest of my life," she said.

The sloppy teenager cleaned up her look and started doing talent contests all over the city. And before long, she was playing with groups and recording songs. Fitzgerald may have been recording as early as 1934 but as a hired hand for a flat fee. Her earliest work was uncredited, and she received no royalties. Her first credited recording session was a song called "I'll Chase the Blues Away," with the Chick Webb Orchestra, in 1935. Chick Webb seems like he was a good man, and he bestowed his knowledge of the music industry upon Fitzgerald. All of that knowledge came in handy because in 1939 Chick Webb died and Fitzgerald, 22, inherited the band. She renamed the group Ella Fitzgerald and Her Famous Orchestra because some asshole kept yelling, "Hey, where the fuck is Chick Webb?"

And that was that. The Boss Lady was in charge. She spent the next several decades touring and recording, both as a solo artist and with people like Louis Armstrong, Mel Tormé, and the Hoboken Heartthrob himself, Frank Sinatra.

In 1941, Fitzgerald made one small personal misstep when she married Benny Kornegay, a longshoreman with a history of dealing drugs. But she soon realized the guy was a bigger red flag than the merch guy for the Dayglo Abortions and the Unabomber combined and got the marriage annulled a year later. And that is why even today people scream, "Benny Kornegay! Benny Kornegay!" when they see a friend talking to some asshole at a bar.

So, the whole fucking Benny Kornegay thing didn't work out but that's OK, because in 1946, while touring with Dizzy Gillespie, Fitzgerald fell in love with the bass player, Ray Brown, and they married. But they both had busy tour schedules and careers to follow, so they split amicably in 1952 and remained in touch. That relationship wasn't perfect, but it wasn't exactly a fucking Benny Kornegay situation, either. And something came out of it that propelled Fitzgerald's career. Brown introduced Fitzgerald to record producer and manager Norman Granz, who took her on as his main client. Granz knew how to work the business and lifted her status up a level or two.

Granz kept her on the road 40 to 45 weeks a year. One shitty tour story—that would make even the worst Nausea tour story sound not so bad—occurred in 1954, when Granz booked Fitzgerald's first tour of Australia. The flight was from Honolulu to Sydney. Granz arranged expensive first-class tickets for the group, but after boarding the Pan-American Airlines flight, Fitzgerald, her piano player, and her assistant were ordered off the plane because they were Black. Granz, who was white, stepped forward to object and they threw him off, too. To make things worse, their luggage remained on the plane, all the way to Sydney. The unfortunate foursome was stuck in Honolulu for three days without a change of clothing until they found another flight to Sydney. They missed the first two concerts of the tour, but by the time they caught up with their luggage, it was tanned and rested.

This wasn't the only instance when Granz made it clear that he wasn't going to put up with discrimination. On October 7, 1955, in Dallas (sometimes reported as Houston), Granz was so vocal about the inequities in American society that the police raided the group's dressing room, fishing for any reason to bust them. There the cops discovered the horror of two men playing dice. They arrested the entire touring party. Incredibly, at the police station, the racist cops asked Fitzgerald for an autograph, proving that the San Francisco punk band War Zone's song "Racists are Dumb Shits" would have sounded awesome back in 1955.

But more importantly, Granz found Fitzgerald better material to record. Up until then, a lot of her recordings were regarded as pop fluff at best or novelty songs at worst. Granz knew how to build a brand. The main thing he did for Fitzgerald's career was to get her to record a series of albums by the best songwriters of the era. Between 1956 and 1964, Fitzgerald recorded the music of Irving Berlin, Duke Ellington, Rodgers and Hart, Cole Porter, and more. Fitzgerald took these songs and made them her own. These are the songs she is best known for, the ones you hear in movies and on TV shows and in restaurants with real silverware and servers named Blaine. These recordings and the bulk of Fitzgerald's artifacts have been preserved by the Smithsonian Institution and the Library of Congress.

In the 1980s Fitzgerald's health began a measured decline. She had a quintuple coronary bypass in 1986; doctors replaced one heart valve. And she was diagnosed with diabetes, which slowly robbed her of sight. She continued recording until 1990. Her last concert was in 1993 at Carnegie Hall. The diabetes worsened; in 1993 she had both legs amputated below the knee. The woman who spent most of her life in the spotlight was rarely seen in public; the 79-year-old died in her Beverly Hills home on June 15, 1996.

WHAT TO CHECK OUT:

Lullabies of Birdland (1954)

Ella Fitzgerald Sings the Cole Porter Song Book (1956)

Ella Fitzgerald Sings the Duke Ellington Song Book (1957)

The Complete Ella Fitzgerald & Louis Armstrong on Verve (1997; recorded 1956–1957)

The Very Best of Ella Fitzgerald (2001)

Gillespie, Dizzy

October 21, 1917–January 6, 1993

MAIN INSTRUMENT: Trumpet

TIME IN THE SCENE: 1935–1992

GENRE: Bebop, Afro-Cuban jazz

NOTABLE QUOTABLE: "Thank you ladies and gentlemen, for your magnificent indifference."

SCENE CRED:

With his trademark beret and horn-rimmed glasses, Dizzy Gillespie's look was just as recognizable as his lightning-quick, zigzagging, divebombing playing style. His cheeks could expand to enormous size, like a pufferfish. And he played an unusual, custom-made trumpet, bent upward at a 45-degree angle. There's a good story about that, which we'll get to. Audiences and bandmates loved his offbeat sartorial choices and his wacky humor, which earned him his moniker, Dizzy.

In 1964, Gillespie ran as an independent candidate for president. He chose the eccentric, cackling comedian Phyllis Diller as his running mate. If elected, he promised to make Miles Davis the head of the C.I.A. and Max Roach, the drummer who punched poor Ornette Coleman, the secretary of defense. Yes, I would have voted for him. He and Charlie Parker, who often got irritated by Dizzy's clowning, practically invented bebop. So how did Dizzy become Dizzy?

He was born John Birks Gillespie in 1917, in Cheraw, South Carolina, the youngest of nine children. His father, James, worked as a mason in the day and a bandleader at night. Instruments were always around the house and his father was happy to teach. By the age of four, young Gillespie took to the piano.

"Learn to play the piano, man, and then you can figure out crazy solos of your own."

Sadly, the elder Gillespie died when John was just 10. He began teaching himself trumpet and trombone. One night the young Gillespie heard jazz pioneer Roy Eldridge on the radio and immediately knew he wanted to be a professional jazz musician. The Eldridge influence was powerful: Gillespie would be compared to Eldridge for the rest of his life, and he was fine with that. Even early on, Gillespie's gift for music was apparent, and he was admitted to the Laurinburg Institute, a historic Black prep school in North Carolina, to study music.

After two years at Laurinburg, when Gillespie was 18, his family moved to Philadelphia. He secured his first professional music gig in 1935, playing trumpet with a group called the Frank Fairfax Orchestra. (Bands didn't really have cool names like the Fried Abortions and the Dayglo Abortions until the 1980s.)

In Philadelphia, Gillespie made his first recording with the Orchestra, a little number called "King Porter Stomp," a song with much less profanity than "Meatmen Stomp."

And Philadelphia is where Gillespie acquired the famous nickname he'd use professionally for the rest of his life. But, as was bound to happen, Gillespie moved to New York City, arriving in 1937, just 20 years old and full of ideas. During his years in New York, he jumped around from band to band, playing with legends like Ella Fitzgerald, Duke Ellington, and Cab Calloway.

Strangely, Gillespie and Calloway did not mesh. Calloway didn't understand the trumpet player's busy, unpredictable style and called it "Chinese music," whatever that's supposed to mean. He also could not tolerate Gillespie's zany antics, leading to what serious jazz scholars ominously refer to as "The Spitball Incident."

In 1941, somebody hit Calloway with a spitball. Some versions of this story say the incident occurred during a practice. Bass Player Milt Hinton claims it was during a concert. In any case, somebody hit Cab Calloway with a spitball, and he was pissed. Gillespie was already on Calloway's shitlist and was the joker in the band, so naturally Cab pointed the finger at him.

This could have been the end of the situation, but Calloway wouldn't let it go, saying, "You did it! I was looking right at you when you threw it!"

Gillespie swore it wasn't him. Hinton backed up the story. But the situation escalated.

Gillespie, who really was innocent this time, said to Calloway, "You're just a damn liar for saying I did it," and Calloway, a big guy who learned to fight on the streets of Baltimore, smacked Gillespie in the face. A scuffle ensued, during which the usually easy-mannered Gillespie stabbed Calloway in the leg with a knife. Needless to say, the trumpet player was fired.

But more importantly, Gillespie and Charlie Parker played together in New York, solidifying the bebop template, with their complex rhythms and erratic harmonies that kept listeners guessing. Gillespie understood the significance of their collaboration: "The music of Charlie Parker and me laid a foundation for all the music that is being played now. Our music is going to be the classical music of the future."

The Dizzy Gillespie entry in *The Rough Guide to Jazz* states, "The whole essence of a Gillespie solo was cliff-hanging suspense: the phrases and the angle of the approach were perpetually varied, breakneck runs were followed by pauses, by huge interval leaps, by long, immensely high notes, by slurs and smears and bluesy phrases; he always took listeners by surprise, always shocking them with a new thought."

By 1946, Gillespie was running his own band. He started incorporating bits of flavor from Brazilian, Caribbean, and Cuban music into his uniquely American bebop. The new blend was dubbed Afro-Cuban jazz. The finest example of Gillespie's Afro-Cuban era is "A Night in Tunisia," a sexy song that became a jazz staple, covered many times over the decades.[10] Gillespie was happier being the bandleader. He could solo however he wanted and cut up onstage with nobody to scold him. Audiences loved his style and sound.

> "They're not particular about whether you're playing a flatted fifth or a ruptured 129th as long as they can dance to it."

The late 1940s to mid-1950s were a robust era for the whimsical jazz genius. A happy accident in 1953 changed his look and sound. During a birthday party for his wife at a Manhattan jazz club called Snookie's, a comedy duo called, wonderfully, Stump and Stumpy, were horsing around and fell on Gillespie's trumpet, bending it to a 45-degree angle. Gillespie picked it up, played it, and liked the sound.

He asked the Martin Band Instrument Company if they could make him a bent trumpet and it became his trademark. That trumpet sold in 1995 at a charity auction for $63,000.

Within a few years of the bent trumpet incident, Gillespie passed his creative peak, as many of the jazz greats did, but he continued playing and recording until he couldn't.

In December 1991, Gillespie had to stop a show in Emeryville, California, because he was feeling ill. He played the next night and then canceled the rest of the tour. He was diagnosed with pancreatic cancer. In 1992, Dizzy got back up onstage a couple

10 You may remember Clair and Cliff Huxtable arguing about when "A Night in Tunisia" was recorded in an episode of *The Cosby Show*. As usual, Clair was right.

more times, yielding a couple of live albums. But on November 26, 1992, he had to cancel what would have been his 33rd performance at Carnegie Hall because he was not well enough to attend. About five weeks later, he was dead at 75. His professional music career lasted nearly 60 years; his catalog of recordings is not only mammoth but momentous.

> "Some days you get up and put the horn to your chops and it sounds pretty good, and you win. Some days you try, and nothing works and the horn wins. This goes on and on and then you die and the horn wins."

WHAT TO CHECK OUT:

Bird and Diz (1950)

Horn of Plenty (1952)

Jazz at Massey Hall (1953)

Groovin' High (1955)

Holiday, Billie

April 7, 1915–July 17, 1959

MAIN INSTRUMENT: Vocals

TIME IN THE SCENE: 1930–1959

GENRE: Jazz, swing

NOTABLE QUOTABLE: "When I sing it, it affects me so
  much I get sick. It takes all the strength out of me."

SCENE CRED:

Poor Billie Holiday. Born with one foot in dog shit and the other
in broken glass, constantly making terrible decisions. It was
never going to end well for her. But maybe all of that dog shit
and broken glass is what helped her to dig so deep and produce
such rich music.

A lot of what should be basic facts in the Billie Holiday story are murky. For example, one source—just one that I know of—lists her birth name as Elinore Harris. But most agree it was Eleanora Fagan. She was born to an unwed teenage couple in Philadelphia in 1915. Her mother, 16-year-old Julia Fagan, was white and of Irish descent. Her father is said to be 18-year-old Clarence Halliday, a Black man. But her birth certificate lists her father as Frank DeViese, whoever that is. Clarence Halliday is the man she knew as a father, whenever he was around. Honestly, both of her parents were shitballs. Clarence Halliday, a fucking banjo player, abandoned the family to become a traveling musician, although he'd pop up every now and then. Julia Fagan took her baby to live with relatives in Baltimore but wasn't very good at parenting, so Eleanora was mostly raised by family. Eleanora skipped school, got in trouble, and by age 9 made her first court appearance. She dropped out of school entirely by age 11 and nobody said shit. Around the time Eleanora quit school, Julia Fagan walked in on a neighbor trying to rape the 11-year-old. The neighbor was arrested, the State of Maryland took custody of Eleanora, and Julia Fagan disappeared to New York to do who-knows-what. After a year in state care, Eleanora, then 12, got released, moved to New York City to reconnect with her crappy mother, and started working in a brothel. She was arrested for prostitution when she was 15.

But I reckon the brothel ultimately had a positive effect on Eleanora, because that's where she was exposed to jazz and blues. And after getting busted for doing one job, she thought she'd give singing a shot instead.

> "I guess I'm not the only one who heard their first good jazz in a whorehouse. But I never tried to make anything of it. If I'd heard Louis and Bessie at a Girl Scout jamboree, I'd have loved it just the same."

The 15-year-old started working in clubs. And started drinking. This is when she began using her professional name, Billie Holiday, taking "Billie" from the name of popular actress Billie Dove and reworking her banjo-strumming father's last name, Halliday, into "Holiday." I have to say, in comparison, the Billie Holiday origin story makes the GG Allin "my dad made me wear a dress and dig my own grave in the basement" story seem kind of quaint.

When the young singer was starting out, a club owner told her that she didn't look Black enough. He suggested wearing blackface. Amazingly, Holiday went along with this absurdity, but only for a short time before she put her foot down.

In 1932, record producer and talent agent John Hammond caught Holiday's set by mistake. He thought the featured act was singer Monette Moore, but when Holiday came onstage, she grabbed his attention. And soon he arranged to have her sing on a record with the popular bandleader Benny Goodman. The record, released in 1933, only sold 300 copies. Undaunted, they made another record, which sold 5,000 copies, a hit by 1930s jazz label metrics. Hammond said, "She was the first girl singer I'd come across who actually sang like an improvising jazz genius."

Around this time, she met the sweet, smart, sharp-dressed saxophone player Lester Young, who gave her the title "Lady Day." They remained lifelong friends and confidants.

Manager Hammond got Billie signed to Brunswick Records, but not as a solo artist, as accompaniment to pianist Teddy Wilson. The record sold an impressive 15,000 copies, but Hammond signed a lousy deal. Instead of royalties, he asked for a one-time flat payment. Artistically, however, the song was a step in the right direction. Billie found her niche, the style she'd play all the way to the grave. She became a torch singer, belting out songs of lost love and romantic frustration. With few exceptions, these melancholy tunes would be her oeuvre.

When she was about 21, Hammond found Holiday another label, Vocalion Records, a subsidiary of the Aeolian Piano Company. Really. When they weren't making pianos, they put out a few records. Actually, Vocalion put out some great stuff—I mean, for a piano company. Seriously, they did, like Louis Armstrong and the master of the Delta blues, Robert Johnson. Vocalion specialized in what the music industry back then called "race records," by which they specifically meant the Black race. Why they didn't just say Black records, I have no idea. Why did a club owner ask Billie Holiday to perform in blackface? That was the America Holiday faced a mere 70 years after slavery.

> "You can be up to your boobies in white satin, with gardenias in your hair and no sugar cane for miles, but you can still be working on a plantation."

By this time, Holiday was on her third or fourth record label. But the labels weren't paying much. The real money in music back then was in live performance. It was better money, but it wasn't easy money. The country was still segregated. Touring was primitive. The American highway system didn't even break ground until 1956. And there was no Taco Bell.

Nonetheless, Billie Holiday and her ethereal voice got a huge break, a gig touring with Count Basie, one of the top cats in jazz. Basie made it a point to give her songs that would fit her sound and allow her to be herself. "She knew how she wanted to sound, and you couldn't tell her what to do," Basie said. Eventually, she was fired. Bandmates said she was temperamental and complained a lot, though this may be chalked up to the misogynistic attitudes of the time.

But without missing a beat, she joined up with the all-white Artie Shaw band. An all-white band fronted by a Black woman was almost unheard of, and their tour of the segregated American South in 1938 was full of tension. In Louisville, Kentucky, a livid Holiday had to be escorted from the stage after some knob job shouted a predictable racial slur. But the shows with high-profile bandleaders like Artie Shaw and Count Basie made Holiday's professional value rise. By the end of 1938, Billie Holiday was practically a household name. And by 1939, that status would be solidified with a single song.

The song "Strange Fruit" has been called the beginning of the civil rights movement. It began as a poem called "Bitter Fruit," published in January 1937 in *New York Teacher*, a magazine published by the New York State Teachers' Association. The author was Abel Meeropol, a communist Jewish teacher from the Bronx. The poem describes the scene of a lynching in an eerie way, comparing the hanging man to fruit on a tree. Meeropol, perhaps fearing reprisal, published under the name Lewis Allan.

If Meeropol intended to keep his identity secret, he did a shitty job, because soon he changed the title to "Strange Fruit," set the poem to music, and started belting it out at union meetings. Then his wife, Laura Duncan, got in on the act. Soon, the two of them were playing their powerful song to packed houses at Madison Square Garden. The peculiar song with the chilling lyrics became a local phenomenon.

The owner of a nightclub called Café Society told Holiday it was the perfect song for her, but she wasn't sure. She was afraid the song would make her the target of racists. But with a little coaxing, Holiday took the song and tooled it to fit her vocal style and unique phrasing. And she worked up a bit of stagecraft to go with it, involving a single white spotlight. At the end of the song, the stage went black. Holiday left the stage in darkness, and a moment later the spotlight returned to an empty stage. The simple, dramatic trick brought the house down. She worked Café Society for two years straight, based on the strength of the act.

"I opened Café Society as an unknown," Holiday said. "I left two years later a star."

Oddly, Holiday said her motivation for doing the song night after night was her deadbeat, banjo-playing dad, Clarence Halliday. Halliday wasn't lynched but he may as well have been. During World War I, Halliday was exposed to mustard gas, which led to breathing issues. Years later, while touring Texas with his banjo, he became ill with a lung disorder and was refused treatment at a local hospital because of his race. By the time he was admitted to a veteran's hospital, it was too late to do anything. Holiday later said of "Strange Fruit," "It still depresses me every time I sing it, though. It reminds me of how Pop died. But I have to keep singing it, not only because people ask for it but because, 20 years after Pop died, the things that killed him are still happening in the South."

In 1939, Holiday's label, Columbia Records, was too conservative to touch the political song. Commodore Records, an independent label, said they'd release it, and it became a macabre hit. It sold more than a million copies. Holiday appeared on the cover of *Time*. The magazine feature sold records and got people talking about civil rights.

In 2015, Johann Hari, author of *Chasing the Scream: The First and Last Days of the War on Drugs*, put forth a theory that this song landed Billie Holiday on a government harassment list. Hari espouses that Harry Anslinger, the commissioner of the U.S. Treasury Department's Federal Bureau of Narcotics, was a racist, hell-bent on destroying Billie Holiday after hearing "Strange Fruit." Supposedly, Holiday received a letter from the Federal Bureau of Narcotics warning her never to play the song again. I fail to see how any song falls under the jurisdiction of the Treasury Department or how "Strange Fruit" has anything to do with narcotics. Holiday wasn't even using narcotics yet. Nonetheless, after "Strange Fruit," Billie Holiday started getting arrested a lot.

The year after "Strange Fruit" started selling like crazy, Holiday's crappy mom, Julia Fagan, asked to borrow money to open a restaurant. Continuing in the ongoing series of bad decisions that would define her very existence, Holiday gave her the money. And in order to capitalize on the success of the kid she'd neglected for years, Julia Fagan named her restaurant Mom Holiday's. Holiday recalled, "I needed some money one night and I knew Mom was sure to have some, so I walked in the restaurant like a stockholder and asked. Mom turned me down flat. She wouldn't give me a cent."

Around this time, Billie Holiday started shooting heroin. She also married the first of her three husbands, all of whom were physically abusive. Abusive husband number one was a trombone player named Jimmy Monroe. While married to Monroe, Holiday began cheating on him with—get this—her drug dealer. Holiday divorced the abusive tromboner in 1947 and married drug dealer/trumpet player Joe Guy in 1951. Yup, that's his fucking name—Joe Guy. What a tool.

Professionally, Holiday excelled. From 1945 through 1947, she raked in a quarter of a million dollars. But she spent $500 a week on heroin, sometimes more. Nonetheless, the hits and tours kept coming.

In May 1947, Holiday was arrested for possession of heroin. Holiday wrote, "It was called 'The United States of America versus Billie Holiday.' And that's just the way it felt." Her own lawyer didn't even bother to show up in court. Holiday, dehydrated and going through heroin withdrawal in the courtroom, begged to be released to a hospital. Instead, she was sentenced to one year and one day at Alderson Federal Prison Camp in West Virginia. She was released a little early, in March 1948, for good behavior. The prison time cost her some career momentum, particularly the suspension of her New York City cabaret card, meaning that she could not perform anywhere in the city where alcohol was sold. She sold tons of records, but her royalty payments were not as frequent nor as large as they should have been. Losing the cabaret card was a huge restriction on her earning potential.

"In this country, don't forget, a habit is no damn private hell," she said. "There's no solitary confinement outside of jail. A habit is hell for those you love. And in this country it's the worst kind of hell for those who love you."

Days after getting out of prison, Holiday played a sold-out comeback show at Carnegie Hall. Billie Holiday was back—but only momentarily, because on January 22, 1949, she was arrested again in San Francisco with a small amount of opium. A couple of weeks earlier, she had been arrested for a fistfight in a nightclub in Los Angeles. The charges for both incidents were dropped, but it wasn't good publicity.

Over the next few years, many of her early records went out of print and royalty payments dried up. Live performance was nearly her entire income.

In 1956, Holiday released her autobiography, *Lady Sings the Blues*. An autobiography should be considered a primary research document. But calling *Lady Sings the Blues* an autobiography is a bit of a stretch. The book was written entirely by a man named William Dufty after just a few conversations with her. And Holiday claimed never to have read the finished book. Some jazz scholars say that the book is mostly accurate, getting the major events right. Others say that it was hastily composed with input from an unreliable narrator. It is worth reading for Holiday's opinions, although some of the facts may be fuzzy or exaggerated.

To co-promote with the book, Holiday simultaneously released a new album, also titled *Lady Sings the Blues*. The new album had four new songs and eight re-recordings of her hits. Somehow, this late in her career, at a time when her style of jazz was basically a nostalgia act, the new album was great. Her voice was in top form and the performance is dramatic. *Lady Sings the Blues* is the Holiday album I reach for most often. On the strength of the book and new album, Holiday played two sold-out shows at Carnegie Hall. And Lady Day seemed happy onstage.

Nat Hentoff, a writer for *DownBeat Magazine*, wrote that Holiday had "a palpable eagerness to reach and touch the audience. And there was mocking wit. A smile was often lightly evident on her lips and her eyes as if, for once, she could accept the fact that there were people who did dig her."

Seventeen years after "Strange Fruit," Holiday was having a moment in the spotlight. Her professional life was getting back on track, but her personal life remained tumultuous. She cheated on her husband/drug dealer Joe Guy with a mafia enforcer named Louis McKay. Predictably, Holiday and McKay were soon arrested for narcotics. Somehow they beat the charges. Holiday divorced Guy and married the mafia tough guy in Mexico.

In the late 1950s, Holiday's world tumbled fast. In 1958 her royalties were just $11. Her careless lawyer only copyrighted two of her many songs. By 1959, jazz was Dave Brubeck, Miles Davis, Ornette Coleman, and Charles Mingus. Billie Holiday could still pack a hall once in a while, but her music was from another era. She never even considered breaking any new ground. Her audiences were getting old, and her body was falling apart.

In early 1959, doctors told Holiday she had cirrhosis. They begged her to stop drinking, and she did for a short while, but then relapsed. She lost a lot of weight. On May 31, 1959, she was admitted to a hospital for treatment of cirrhosis and heart disease. While she was in the hospital, police searched her apartment and found heroin. She was shackled to her hospital bed and placed under the watch of an armed police officer around the clock. The 44-year-old jazz singer died of heart failure on July 17, 1959, handcuffed to a bed. Her bank account balance was just 70 cents because McKay had stolen the rest.

WHAT TO CHECK OUT:

The Complete 1951 Storyville Club Sessions (1951)

Lady Sings the Blues (1956)

Body and Soul (1957)

A Flag for Lady Day (1964)

Kirk, Rahsaan Roland

August 7, 1935–December 5, 1977

MAIN INSTRUMENT: Saxophone, flute, clarinet

TIME IN THE SCENE: 1955–1977

GENRE: Free jazz, soul jazz, hard bop

NOTABLE QUOTABLE: "We are all driven by an invisible whip. Some run, some have fun, some are hip, some tip, some dip, but we all must answer to the invisible whip."

SCENE CRED:

Rahsaan Roland Kirk was freakishly talented, funny, politically outspoken, profound, and a true weirdo. He and a group of like-minded mutants pulled off a series of incendiary pranks against the mass media that would make Crass envious. I almost don't know where to begin.

Just as the guitarist of the Japanese punk band Lip Cream said that their band name came to him "in a dream," dreams would be important to Rahsaan Roland Kirk. He was born in Columbus, Ohio, in 1935 as Ronald Theodore Kirk, but he dreamed that he should transpose a couple of letters in his first name and become Roland Kirk. In 1970, he saw the word Rahsaan in another dream and added it to his name.

Between those two dreams, he had another dream in which he was playing two saxophones at once. He recalled, "I dreamed that I was playing two horns at once and I decided to do it. My life has been motivated by dreams. I have had a series of dreams throughout my life, and each one I had changed my life. That's why I added Rahsaan to my name. I'm not a Muslim."

That's right, Kirk's claim to fame is that he could play two or three instruments at a time. And he was blind. Kirk lost his sight when he was two years old. His parents noticed he had vision problems and took him to a hospital, where he was given a heavy dosage of eye drops that only made things worse. Eventually, he lost his sight completely. Eye problems would continue to bedevil him for the rest of his short life.

As a child, Kirk's first instrument was a common garden hose. When his mom noticed that he was really playing something and not just fucking around, she bought him a bugle. Later, as a professional musician, he would incorporate the garden hose into his act, calling it "the black mystery pipes."

"I didn't ask my mother to buy me a trumpet or a violin. I started right on the water hose."

Kirk studied music at the Ohio State School for the Blind. By the time he was 14, he'd developed a technique for playing three saxophones at once. He modified his instruments to make them easier to play simultaneously. He bent them and explored different types of mouth pieces. He called one of his modified saxophones a "moon zellar," another a "skitch." He could play the flute with his nose and developed a style of singing through a flute that was later appropriated by Ian Anderson of Jethro Tull. He incorporated whistles, alarm clocks, and sirens into his musical arsenal. Obviously, this young man had talent and ideas from another planet.

But Kirk's artistic breakthrough was when he mastered circular breathing, a technique that involves breathing in through the nose while simultaneously pushing air out through the mouth, using air stored in the cheeks. Circular breathing enables a player to play almost continuously without a break. By the time he was 15, he went professional, playing in clubs and going on tour.

In 1955, Kirk knew that he needed to get out of Ohio if he was going to be a working jazz musician. Curiously, instead of moving to New York City like everyone else at the time, he picked Los Angeles. Things didn't work out in LA, so he began heading back to Ohio. In El Paso, he caught up with the big-band leader Count Basie, who, surprisingly, let the 20-year-old sit in with the group. That must have been the strangest Count Basie gig ever. By 1956, Kirk followed the flow for once and moved to New York.

Right away, he signed a record deal for his first album, *Triple Threat*. He picked up work with Charles Mingus, Quincy Jones, and others. But of course, such an unusual individual wouldn't be content as a sideman. He was born to be a bandleader. He called his group the Vibration Society. His explanation for the name was that musical vibrations are what hold all people together, like glue. It was a statement of inclusiveness, an attempt to erase the division between artist and audience. All people were part of the Society.

Unfortunately, Kirk didn't make much of a dent in the jazz market. His records never sold well. He was a cult artist at best. And, naturally, anything as weird as Kirk's music was bound to be divisive; critics thought his playing was a novelty act.

"What about a blues in W, in the key of W?"

But he had fans, too. Fellow musicians recognized Kirk's gift, like saxophone player Hank Crawford, who said, "He would be like this 14-year-old blind kid playing two horns at once. They would bring him out and he would tear the joint up. Now, they had him doing all kinds of goofy stuff, but he was playing the two horns, and he was playing the shit out of them."

And as pianist Larry Willis described one show in New York City, "He came on the bandstand and scared everybody to death.

I saw other horn players putting their instruments back in their cases!"

A deeply knowledgeable player, Kirk had a keen understanding of all eras of jazz. And while his music could get pretty out there, he used a basic hard bop approach as a foundation, from which he built upward and outward. His obituary in the *Washington Post* picked up on that, calling his sound "a splendid blend of the traditional and new."

Oh, yeah. Kirk also didn't like the word "jazz." He preferred his own term, "Black classical music." This is how he explained it: "If you talk with the people of New Orleans, the musicians didn't have a chance to name their music. It was a European that named the music 'jazz.' . . . The only reason I call it Black classical music is because I feel that Milt Jackson, John Coltrane, Sonny Rollins, Ben Webster, Sidney Bechet, Mingus, Coleman Hawkins, Bird, all these people, I feel that they are classics. They are Black classical musicians."

Around the time he made this statement, he took to smashing chairs and burning money onstage, a symbolic repudiation of the norm.

"We're gonna burn it down!"

Kirk's next great idea and loudest political statement came in the summer of 1970. He temporarily suspended his preferred term, Black classical music, to form an activist group called the Jazz & the People's Movement with his friend Mark Davis and an assortment of jazz rebels. Kirk and Davis's source of irritation was that jazz was underrepresented on television. Now, by 1970, jazz in the U.S. was a shadow of what it had been during the big band era or even the cool jazz / West Coast jazz era. The fact that there wasn't much jazz on TV was probably unnoticed by 99 percent of TV viewers. But the Jazz & the People's Movement did raise some valid points.

"You know, man, television's been a closed shop long enough. Networks ain't got no respect for Black musicians, and it's at the point now that they're really suppressing the whole culture," Kirk said. "When was the last time you saw a Black cat playin' on the TV set—other than Louie or Duke or Ella? Don't get me wrong, Duke is the tops. But Black people gotta know their whole music—Black kids gotta know their whole music! Clubs closing all over the place, we need the media outlet more than ever."

The Movement drew up a petition that they circulated around the New York jazz scene with the intention of presenting it to all three TV networks: ABC, NBC, and CBS.

The petition read in part, "Your signature on this petition will be interpreted as an indication of sincere dedication to the struggle to open the media, and to enable Black artists to reach the positions of prominence that their artistry deserves—to breathe new life into Black culture. Failure to sign this petition will be interpreted as signifying your disagreement with and opposition to its fundamental concepts."

The Jazz & the People's Movement also came up with a list of demands for the networks, quoted verbatim here:

1. The establishment of a board of musicians to coordinate the production of three to four jazz specials each season, designed to educate the public about the history of Black music.

2. Increased exposure of Black musicians (both established names and those without wide recognition).

3. Increased employment of Black musicians and technicians throughout the medium.

4. Recognition of talent: acknowledgement for solos, musical arrangements, and members of the staff bands.

5. The option for guest musicians to be interviewed by variety show hosts or participate in discussion panels.

6. Greater promotion of Black art in media and trade advertising.

7. Hiring of Black producers, directors, and talent coordinators at the networks.

Sympathetic jazz clubs let the group hold meetings, each of which attracted up to 150 attendees. Lots of people signed the petition. Kirk, Davis, and the group brainstormed ways to present the petition and demands to the networks. What they came up with was revolutionary.

On August 27, 1970, the Jazz & the People's Movement ambushed *The Merv Griffin Show*. Unfortunately, the show wasn't live, but they made a strong point. Kirk, Davis, and about 50 jazz fans got tickets to the filming and packed the studio audience. When Kirk felt the moment was right, he stood up, pulled a clarinet from his coat, and started wailing away. His 50 conspirators stood up and did the same with their own instruments and whistles. Some of them produced protest signs, bearing slogans like STOP THE WHITEWASH NOW! and HONOR AMERICAN JAZZ MUSIC!

The *Merv Griffin Show* studio band tried to play louder than the jazz upstarts, but they were outnumbered and quickly gave up. Filming was suspended for the day. The producers of the show met with the Jazz & the People's Movement and, unbelievably, had a calm, rational discussion. Griffin's producers promised to make changes to the program. The promises were never met, but it was a start, a minor victory. The unusual protest made local TV news, but the spin was unflattering, labeling the Jazz & the People's Movement "a group of Black militants." Thrilled with any media coverage at all, the Movement began planning their next attack.

On October 1, 1970, Johnny Carson's eighth anniversary as host of *The Tonight Show*, about 50 members of the Movement, again with instruments hidden in their coats, turned up at Rockefeller Plaza under the guise of a church group. One of the members even called ahead and booked a tour of the facilities. After the guided tour, the group positioned itself in front of the studio where *The Tonight Show* was shot. But not having tickets to the filming, they were stopped at the studio doors. So, they staged a sit-in.

Kirk bellowed, "Open that door and let us in or I'll blow it down!" Desperately hoping to deescalate the situation, studio security let Kirk in. Joseph Cuneff, the director of NBC nighttime programming, met with Kirk and the two men discussed the issue lucidly. Kirk said, "I am satisfied with Mr. Cuneff's initial response to our actions."

Two weeks later, the Movement targeted *The Dick Cavett Show*. Unfortunately, Kirk was on tour, so the action was coordinated by Davis and trumpet player Lee Morgan. One of Cavett's guests was the British actor Trevor Howard. Cavett asked Howard what he liked about New York City, and Howard, as if he were in on the plan, provided the perfect opportunity for the Movement to strike.

"I used to simply adore going out at night to the jazz clubs," Howard said. "There were so many! My wife Helen and I could not get enough of that music. But I have certainly noticed the last times I have been here that this aspect of the city has changed. It has certainly been a surprise, and I'm not sure quite how to explain it."

The Movement sprang into action, blowing their horns and whistles for an hour. Dick Cavett covered his ears. While the cacophony raged, Davis, Morgan, and two other Movement leaders met backstage with people from *The Dick Cavett Show* and ABC TV. They negotiated a 15-minute segment on an upcoming episode of the show to discuss their grievances. Two weeks later, members of the Movement, excluding Kirk, who was still on tour, appeared on the show. Cavett was so intrigued by their ideas that he gave them 30 minutes, a huge victory for their cause.

A month later, Kirk was invited to appear on *The Today Show*. Invited. There was no need to invade. Host Hugh Downs gave Kirk time to play and to discuss jazz and the Movement. The discussion was respectful and intelligent.

Downs asked, "Can whites learn to appreciate and to play Black music?"

Kirk responded, "Definitely, definitely. The only [thing] we're saying is that we think the credit should be given to the Black man in this country for what he has contributed. In other words, we credit Bach and Beethoven in Europe with all the beautiful works that they've written, without any qualms. And we figure that the music of Sidney Bechet and Duke Ellington and John Coltrane, all these beautiful people are just like classical musicians in their own right, and we call them Black classical musicians."

For the Movement's final statement, Kirk appeared on *The Ed Sullivan Show* on January 24, 1971. Since 1948, *The Ed Sullivan Show* had been an entertainment institution. The program introduced Elvis Presley and the Beatles to America. And a good performance on *The Ed Sullivan Show* meant that America might let you get to second base, which back then meant sharing a root beer.

Kirk began the live performance by saying, "True Black music will be heard tonight!" Ed Sullivan must have crapped his baggy trousers. This is the guy who had Elvis Presley filmed from the waist up, who told the Rolling Stones they had to change the lyrics to "Let's Spend the Night Together," and who forbade Jim Morrison to use the word "higher."

But the stodgy Sullivan seemed to like it, saying at the conclusion of the set, "That was wonderful! Rahsaan Roland Kirk, ladies and gentlemen!" Even his baggy trousers seemed to like it.

If only it had ended there. Unscripted and unknown to Kirk and Sullivan, the Black comedian Godfrey Cambridge, who was another guest on the show, sneaked up behind Sullivan, crowned him with an outlandish Afro wig, and proclaimed him "an honorary Negro." Needless to say, Rahsaan Roland Kirk did not get to second base with America. The press was not kind to this moment, but Kirk and his conspirators had made their point. The Jazz & the People's Movement disbanded shortly after.

In 1975, Kirk had a stroke that left his body partially paralyzed. Amazingly, he modified his instruments so he could play them with just one arm and was still able to play two horns at once; he continued touring and recording. But on the morning of December 5, 1977, following a gig at Indiana University in Bloomington, the 42-year-old Kirk had a second stroke, which was fatal.

You would think that a blind person who could play multiple instruments at the same time would have become a major musical celebrity, but most people never heard of him.

WHAT TO CHECK OUT:

Triple Threat (1956)

Kirk's Work (1961)

Volunteered Slavery (1969)

Pre-Rahsaan (1978; recorded 1961–1968)

Mingus, Charles

April 22, 1922–January 5, 1979

MAIN INSTRUMENT: Bass, piano

TIME IN THE SCENE: 1943–1979

GENRE: Orchestral jazz, bebop, hard bop, free jazz, third stream, avant-garde jazz

NOTABLE QUOTABLE: "Yeah, I pledge allegiance, to the United States of America. . . . I pledge an allegiance to see that someday they will live up to their promises, to the victims that they call citizens."

SCENE CRED:

I once drove from Austin, Texas, to Monterrey, Mexico, and back, 13 hours round trip, listening to nothing but Charles Mingus. Of course, I once drove from Austin, Texas, to St. Petersburg, Florida, and back, 34 hours round trip, listening to nothing but Black Flag, so I might be damaged.

The Mingus catalog is extensive, rewarding, and unpredictable. You could easily listen to Mingus for 13 hours and not hear a quarter of it. He played on more than 100 albums, including 30 during the 1950s, his most productive decade. And he did it all, from orchestral jazz with Duke Ellington to speedy bebop with Charlie Parker and Dizzy Gillespie to the far-out stuff that came later. But my favorite material falls in the middle of the Mingus timeline, the mid-1950s through early 1960s, when he was running his own bands and constantly looking for something new and original.

"I'm trying to play the truth of what I am. The reason it's difficult is because I'm changing all the time," he said.

Mingus had an eclectic ancestry: Black, Native American, German, Chinese, and possibly Swedish. As he put it, "I am

Charles Mingus. Half-Black man. Yellow man. Half-yellow. Not even yellow, nor white enough to pass for nothing but Black and not too light enough to be called white." He was born in Arizona in 1922 to a military family but was mostly raised in the Watts area of southern Los Angeles. His dad was a tough sergeant in the U.S. Army. In a 1962 interview, Mingus said his father never loved him. "I never had any idea or father image. Anything that was something wrong he knocked it down, you know? I never felt any love in my family. I had no one to say what am I supposed to be like. He never even told me the world like it was. He never said anything about Black or white. He never told me anything."

His mother only allowed gospel music in the house, which would be a consistent element of the Mingus sound, best exemplified in the song "Better Git It in Your Soul" from my favorite of his albums, *Mingus Ah Um*. Young Charles liked gospel, but clandestine moments with the radio turned him on to classical music, which would be another recurring element in his style. And the radio introduced him to jazz during the orchestral era. He fell for the impeccable, erudite Duke Ellington, little knowing that someday Duke would be his boss.

In high school, Mingus started on trombone before switching to cello. He began writing music in his teens, compositions that were a unique blend of classical music and jazz, foreshadowing third stream, a genre that wouldn't exist for another two decades. He briefly considered a career as a concert cellist before coming to the cruel conclusion that classical music career opportunities for Black people were almost zero. He switched to standup bass, using some of the cello techniques he'd learned, and focused on jazz.

By 1943, Mingus was a professional jazz musician, touring and recording with the biggest jazz artists of the time, like Louis

Armstrong, Charlie Parker, and his hero, Duke Ellington. He spent almost a decade learning the inner workings of jazz from the masters, before making the mandatory move to New York City in 1952.

In New York, the bassist found no lack of work or like-minded musicians. He played with Miles Davis, Dizzy Gillespie, Bud Powell, Max Roach, and others. In true do-it-yourself style, Mingus and Roach joined forces to start their own record label, Debut Records, so that they'd have better control over their careers. A secondary directive of their label was to document upcoming musicians who might not otherwise get to record, sort of like Crass Records.

Mingus began his own groups, usually with 8 to 10 people. The blanket name for Mingus's ever-changing group of musicians was the Jazz Workshop. He worked his players hard, like boot camp, like his father probably worked his troops. The artists took to calling it the Jazz Sweatshop. And Mingus was branded with his epithet, the Angry Man of Jazz.

On one occasion, Mingus smashed his expensive bass, the most valuable thing he owned and the tool of his trade, by throwing it off the stage at a heckler. And this was more than two decades before that handsome devil in the Clash smashed his bass onstage at the Palladium. To be honest, the tall, skinny Clash guy probably looked cooler, but Mingus was probably more intense. Mingus was only five foot nine but seemed bigger. He tended towards obesity, especially in his later years, saying, "I eat out of nerves." Even though he could be wickedly funny, he could also be brooding, intimidating, and wrathful.

Once a frustrated Mingus chased everyone except his drummer and guitarist off the stage and played as a trio for 90 minutes before summoning the banished players to return. They were lucky; another time Mingus punched trombone player Jimmy Knepper in the mouth, breaking a tooth and permanently altering his sound. Knepper claimed the punch ruined his embouchure and he could never again play in the high register. He pressed charges against Mingus, but the judge suspended the sentence.

Mingus was prone to violent outbursts and depressive episodes. He had extended periods of creative inspiration followed by long lulls. He voluntarily checked himself into the Bellevue Psychiatric Hospital. Upon his discharge, he recorded the album *The Black Saint and the Sinner Lady*, widely considered one of his best. The album was inspired by his time in Bellevue. Mingus recruited his psychotherapist, Dr. Edmund Pollock, to write the liner notes.

During the 1950s, his most fruitful time, Mingus was on a creative hot streak. The title track of the 1956 album *Pithecanthropus Erectus* is supposed to be a musical timeline of human evolution—a novel idea for a jazz instrumental. The 10-minute song concludes in pandemonium as humans realize they can enslave others. The next year he released the weird and creepy album *The Clown*. The title track is a darkly humorous 12-minute jazz jam, narrated by American humorist Jean Shepherd of *A Christmas Story* fame, about a frustrated clown who dies onstage trying to get applause: "Man, there was this clown!" Again, not normal subject matter for jazz. Maybe for a Dead Kennedys song.

During the Biggest Year in Jazz, 1959, Mingus and his current Jazz Workshop players recorded *Mingus Ah Um*. Every song on this record is a winner. "Goodbye Pork Pie Hat" is a farewell to the popular and kind saxophone player Lester Young, who'd died recently. "Boogie Stop Shuffle" has a deep groove. And the joyful

"Better Git It in Your Soul" is my favorite number, but "Fables of Faubus" is probably the most important track on the album.

Orval Eugene Faubus, the asshole 36th governor of Arkansas, refused to comply with the 1954 U.S. Supreme Court decision in *Brown v. Board of Education* that made public school segregation illegal. Faubus ordered the Arkansas National Guard to prevent Black students from entering Little Rock Central High. Naturally, the multi-racial Mingus thought this was bullshit and wrote what may have been the first punk song, "Fables of Faubus." The original version of the song had lyrics, which Mingus himself, who was not a singer, intended to sing on the album. Thematically, "Fables of Faubus" would have fit in on *In God We Trust, Inc.*

> "Oh, Lord, don't let 'em shoot us!
> Oh, Lord, don't let 'em stab us!
> Oh, Lord, no more swastikas!
> Oh, Lord, no more Ku Klux Klan!
>
> Name me someone who's ridiculous, Dannie,
> Governor Faubus!
>
> Why is he so sick and ridiculous?
> He won't permit integrated school.
>
> Then he's a fool! Boo! Nazi fascist supremacists!
> Boo! Ku Klux Klan with your Jim Crow plan.
>
> Name me a handful that's ridiculous, Dannie.
> Faubus, Rockefeller, Eisenhower.
> Why are they so sick and ridiculous?
>
> Two, four, six, eight:
> They brainwash and teach you hate.
> H-E-L-L-O, hello."

Now, re-read those lyrics in your best Jello Biafra voice. These potent words worried the chickenshit conformist executives at Columbia Records, who wanted to sell records but not make people think about anything unpleasant. They told Mingus the song could go on the album as an instrumental. Amazingly, he didn't have to change the title. A year later, Mingus re-recorded the song with vocals for the album *Charles Mingus Presents Charles Mingus* on the independent label Candid Records, who were no chickenshit conformists. Mingus would continue to play the song, often with his jagged lyrics, in concert for years.

Between touring and recording, the unconventional Mingus published a pamphlet, *The Charles Mingus CAT-alog for Toilet Training Your Cat*, which he sold through the mail. The four-step program promises to have your cat weaned off the litter box and using a toilet, just like you, in a couple of weeks. Here's one tip from the *CAT-alog*: "Don't be surprised if you hear the toilet flush in the middle of the night. A cat can learn how to do it, spurred on by his instinct to cover up. His main thing is to cover up. If he hits the flush knob accidentally and sees that it cleans the bowl inside, he may remember and do it intentionally."

The pamphlet became an unexpected hit among jazz collectors and cat owners. It's been bootlegged several times, but an authorized reproduction is being sold online today for just 10 bucks.

Mingus rounded out the 1950s and 1960s with many more albums, but he was slowing down. Mental and physical health issues slowed his productivity. The gritty documentary *Mingus: Charlie Mingus 1968* shows him playing live, working on music, and firing a .410 shotgun into the ceiling of his New York apartment. It also shows him being evicted for nonpayment of rent. Despite being a world-famous jazz musician, Mingus couldn't keep a roof over his head. Late in his career, though, he received grants from the National Endowment for the Arts, the Smithsonian Institute, and the Guggenheim Foundation, which helped his finances somewhat. He was married four times and had five children.

Mingus published his autobiography, *Beneath the Underdog: His World as Composed by Mingus*, in 1971. Like a lot of autobiographies, Mingus's book has been picked apart for including fuzzy dates and events that may have happened differently or not at all, but it is probably the best source of information about the man.

> "My book was written for Black people, to tell them how to get through life. I was trying to upset the white man in it."

In 1977, Mingus was diagnosed with amyotrophic lateral sclerosis, also known as Lou Gehrig's disease. He needed to use a wheelchair and could no longer play his huge upright bass, but he continued to compose on the piano. A couple of years later, Mingus traveled to Mexico, seeking alternative medical treatment for his ALS. The 56-year-old Angry Man of Jazz died on January 5, 1979. His last wife, Susan, scattered his ashes in the Ganges River.

WHAT TO CHECK OUT:

Pithecanthropus Erectus (1956)

The Clown (1957)

Mingus Ah Um (1959)

Mingus Dynasty (1960)

The Black Saint and the Sinner Lady (1963)

Mingus Mingus Mingus Mingus Mingus (1964)

Monk, Thelonious

October 10, 1917–February 17, 1982

MAIN INSTRUMENT: Piano

TIME IN THE SCENE: 1940–1973

GENRE: Bebop

NOTABLE QUOTABLE: "There are no wrong notes; some are just more right than others."

SCENE CRED:

Thelonious Sphere Monk was an oddball, even in the odd world of jazz. But with a birth name like that, he might not have had much choice. I'd say they broke the mold after Monk, but *what* fucking mold?

"Everyone is a genius at being themselves."

Monk was a kooky dresser. He wore strange sunglasses and a goatee when such a look was just fucking weird. About a decade later, the beatniks nabbed his style. He said bizarre things, like "It's always night, or we wouldn't need light" and "You've got to dig it to dig it, you dig?"

And he loved hats. Berets from France. Fur hats from Finland. Silk skullcaps from Asia. Fedoras, trilbies, and bobbles. And in his later years as a recluse, he favored a dingy baseball cap.

He had small hands and an unorthodox way of playing the keys, with his fingers held flat instead of curved. He used his fingers like hammers and really hit the keys hard. That is, when he hit them at all. He was prone to leaving unpredictable gaps in his music for dramatic effect.

"The loudest noise in the world is silence."

He played dissonant notes, making the music seem jagged. He switched keys abruptly. The owner of one New York record store, who refused to carry his titles, said Monk had "two left hands." And even though he was at the birth of bebop, he watched Charlie Parker and Dizzy Gillespie soar while critics and fans were slow to pick up on his style. Jazz critic Philip Larkin called Monk "the elephant on the keyboard."

When the mood struck him, Monk would rise from his piano seat, shuffle his feet, and twirl around in little circles while the rest of the band carried on. Sometimes he'd fall asleep at the piano or just stare into space without playing a note. Or he might just wander away from the piano and out of the club to do something else.

Over a 43-year career, Monk composed about 70 songs—not very prolific—but many of them, like "'Round Midnight" and "Straight, No Chaser," became jazz classics, staples of the genre, which have been recorded again and again by his successors. Within the genre, only Duke Ellington and his thousands of songs have been more widely recorded.

> "Where's jazz going? I don't know. Maybe it's going to hell. You can't make anything go anywhere. It just happens."

Monk was born in 1917 in Rocky Mount, North Carolina. The family moved to New York when he was five. He started playing piano a year later, under the guidance of his mother and a neighbor. Formal lessons began at age 10 with a teacher who pushed classical playing. After a couple of years of classical piano lessons, it was apparent to the haughty teacher that Monk's real interest was Fats Waller and Duke Ellington; classes were canceled.

Monk's professional music career began when he was 14, playing at rent parties in Harlem and amateur nights at the Apollo Theater. Monk was quickly barred from amateur night because he was too good. So, he did the next logical thing—to his thinking, at least—and went on tour with a faith healer. He was 17 years old, living on the road.

When he returned from tour, Monk became the house pianist at Minton's Playhouse, a Manhattan nightclub where jazz musicians met to trade licks onstage and to talk music. Charlie Parker, Dizzy Gillespie, and Miles Davis were all regulars at Minton's. John Coltrane said, "Monk is exactly the opposite of Miles. He talks about music all the time, and he wants so much for you to understand that if, by chance, you ask him something, he'll spend hours if necessary to explain it to you."

Monk's quirkiness kept him stateside during World War II. At his induction, an army psychiatrist branded him a "psychiatric reject," and he was excused from service.

"Sometimes it's to your advantage for people to think you're crazy."

In 1944, Monk had his first recording session, backing up tenor saxophone player Coleman Hawkins, who raved about the unconventional piano player. In 1947, Monk signed to Blue Note Records and started making albums with his own name on the cover. Alfred Lion, co-owner of Blue Note, was an early Monk fan. He didn't care if the records made money or lost money; he just wanted them out. You'd think that being on Blue Note, the top label in jazz, would have made Monk a star overnight, but it didn't happen that way. In February 1948, one of Monk's supporters helped him secure a week of gigs at the stalwart

Village Vanguard, but not a single person came. Talk about a Spinal Tap moment! Monk stayed with Blue Note for five years.

In 1947, Monk married his neighborhood sweetheart, Nellie Smith, who looked after her eccentric husband. Monk avoided heroin, but at this time he was drinking alcohol, taking sleeping pills, popping Dexedrine, and consuming whatever else looked interesting. Monk needed a caretaker to steer him away from misadventure.

Although Monk had his supporters among musicians and a few dedicated fans, his career was not great. In 1951, when it looked like things couldn't get worse, things got worse. Monk and fellow jazz pianist Bud Powell were caught with a little bit of heroin. It was Powell's. Monk didn't touch heroin, but he took the rap and served 60 days in jail. But the worst of the worst was that his cabaret card, a license to play music in New York bars, was revoked for six years. It was the same heavy blow dealt to Billie Holiday in 1948. Monk's earning potential was greatly decreased. He still made records and toured, but being virtually banned in New York was practically a death sentence for a jazz musician.

Fortunately, Monk acquired a fan and powerful ally in 1954 when he met Baroness Pannonica de Koenigswarter, a member of the unbelievably wealthy Rothschild family, and a genuine fucking baroness. The baroness liked jazz. She picked Thelonious Monk and Charlie Parker as her personal projects and gave them money, legal assistance, rides to the doctor, and more. The baroness and Nellie Smith worked as a team to keep Monk's life on track.

In 1957, the baroness succeeded in getting Monk's valuable cabaret card restored. Using medical records and character references, she convinced the police that Monk wasn't a junkie.

But on October 15, 1958, the baroness was driving Monk to a week-long residency at a club in Baltimore when they stopped at a motel and asked for a drink of water. The manager of the motel thought there was something dangerous about Monk and called the police.

By the time the police arrived, Monk was in the back seat of the baroness's Bentley. Monk refused to exit the vehicle and grabbed the steering wheel to anchor himself. Police beat his hands with nightsticks until he relented. Some of the lumps never went away.

The cops found some narcotics in a suitcase in the trunk, and the pair was arrested. The judge threw out the case, declaring that the detention was unwarranted and the search was made under duress. But word of the bust reached authorities in New York City, who again suspended Monk's cabaret card.

Monk continued on his own path, playing where and when he could and recording. Record sales were never strong; his music was deemed too unusual for the mainstream. Somehow, Monk got signed to Columbia Records, where Miles Davis became a rich man. But there would never be Ferraris and Lamborghinis for Monk. However, Columbia, one of the biggest record labels in the world, put their faith and money into promoting Monk. His first album for Columbia, *Monk's Dream*, released in 1963, became his best-selling album.

"Trying to explain music is like trying to dance architecture."

Monk got another little career boost when he appeared on the cover of *Time* in 1964. The article, "The Loneliest Monk," written by Barry Farrell, does an excellent job of capturing the Monk mystique. A bit of it reads, "Monk's sound is so obviously his own that to imitate it would be as risky and embarrassing as affecting a Chinese accent when ordering chop suey. . . . Though Monk's career has been painful and often thankless, it has also been a tortoise-and-hare race with flashier, more ingratiating men—many of whom got lost in narcotic fogs, died early in squalor and disgrace or abandoned their promise, to fall silent on their horns."

Monk experienced bouts of depression as far back as the 1940s, when psychiatric care was not as advanced as it is today. He was institutionalized several times, beginning in 1956. During one stay at Grafton State Hospital in Massachusetts, he was given the powerful antipsychotic Thorazine, a drug primarily used in the treatment of schizophrenia. He may not have needed it, and it may have done him more harm than good. By the late 1960s, his mental health was in sharp decline. He'd have a few days of intense activity followed by silent withdrawal into himself. Doctors wanted to try electroconvulsive therapy, but the family was against the idea. He was given more drugs instead. An exact diagnosis was never determined, and by the mid-1970s, Monk was a virtual recluse.

Monk spent the last six years of his life in the home of his patron, Baroness Pannonica de Koenigswarter, in New Jersey. The baroness and Nellie tended to his needs. He had few visitors and played no music. On February 17, 1982, the 64-year-old co-architect of bebop died of a stroke.

Thelonious Monk summed up his life and his playing with these spare words: "I say, play your own way."

WHAT TO CHECK OUT:

Genius of Modern Music: Volume 1 (1951)

Genius of Modern Music: Volume 2 (1952)

Monk's Music (1957)

Monk's Dream (1963)

Morgan, Lee

July 10, 1938–February 19, 1972

MAIN INSTRUMENT: Trumpet

TIME IN THE SCENE: 1956–1972

GENRE: Bebop, hard bop

NOTABLE QUOTABLE: "It's all music. It's either hip or it ain't."

SCENE CRED:

Lee Morgan's all-too-short life had its ups and downs. He was on a nice little up when it all came down. His trumpet playing has been called funky, soulful, bright, sassy, bluesy, and brash. More than once his sound has been likened to the Godfather of Soul, James Brown. He had confidence and charisma. He dressed smartly and had a nice smile.

Trumpet player Freddie Hubbard, Morgan's peer, said he was "the only young cat that scared me when he played. He had so much fire and natural feeling." Even the biggest name in jazz, Miles Davis, had to admit, "Lee Morgan was the baddest trumpet player out there. Badder than Diz. Badder than me." He made more than 30 albums in about 16 years.

But there's no way to tell the Lee Morgan story without telling the Helen Moore story. Moore, whose last name has alternately been recorded as More, was born in 1926 on a farm near Shallotte, North Carolina. As of this writing, Shallotte has a little more than 4,000 residents. Who knows if they even counted people there in 1926. By the time she was 13, she had her first child. Another one came a year later.

Motherhood was not what she wanted, especially at such a young age. At 15, she left her two babies to be raised by her grandparents and moved to Wilmington, which had to be more exciting than Shallotte. Soon, she was married to a 39-year-old liquor bootlegger. A couple of years later, her much-older husband drowned in a river. After the funeral, the 19-year-old widow went to visit relatives in New York City, fell in love with the jazz scene, and stayed for 30 years.

About a year before Moore became a mother, Lee Morgan was born in Philadelphia, the youngest of four kids. His sister Ernestine gave him his first trumpet for his 13th birthday, and he took lessons. The Morgans were a stable, loving, respectable, church-going family. Young Lee had his own band by the age of 15; they played the Philadelphia club circuit and got paid.

But things really picked up in the summer of 1956. Morgan, who'd just finished high school, was asked to fill in for two weeks with Art Blakey and the Jazz Messengers at a Philadelphia club. Blakey, 36 years old, was already a seasoned jazz legend and a pioneer of the burgeoning hard bop style.

From the stint with Art Blakey, Morgan jumped to playing with bebop royalty Dizzy Gillespie. Morgan's playing with Gillespie caught the attention of "the animal brothers," Alfred Lion and Francis Wolff of Blue Note Records. The German-Jewish exiles were businessmen, but they were also jazz enthusiasts. They saw both talent and dollars in the 18-year-old and signed him. Within months, Morgan's first solo album, *Indeed!*, was out on the hottest label in jazz and shipping to stores. Not a bad start for the recent high school graduate.

Morgan spent the next couple of years cranking out solo albums—about seven—until he was summoned back to play with Art Blakey and the Jazz Messengers. He could have focused on his solo career, which was picking up steam. But a gig is a gig, as they say, and Morgan returned to the Jazz Messengers while continuing his own solo work.

If Morgan had said no, his life might have turned out very differently, because Blakey had a predatorial way of keeping musicians in the band for next to nothing. He got them hooked on heroin and paid them in drugs.

"I'll have you guys turned on in two weeks," Blakey told Morgan and another new recruit. And that's exactly what happened. Somehow, perhaps with his years of experience with the needle, Blakey was able to keep his habit under control while simultaneously controlling his younger, weaker band members. At least the music was good. In 1958, the 19-year-old Morgan played on the Art Blakey album *Moanin'*, probably the best example of the hard bop sound. Onstage, the crusty Blakey would encourage his young trumpet wonder, shouting, "Talk to the people, tell them your story!"

By this time, Helen Moore had become a valuable part of the New York jazz scene. The woman who had abandoned two kids in North Carolina found herself mothering the fuckups of jazz in her immaculate New York apartment. She was said to be a wonderful cook and a gracious host. Tattered, hungry jazz musicians could always find food, a shower, and a place to crash with Moore. She mended their worn-out clothes and made phone calls for them. She probably even wiped their asses because, let's face it, most musicians are big fucking babies who only know how to do one specific thing.

Still in 1958, Morgan met a Japanese model, Kiko Yamamoto, and they married after just two weeks. But when Yamamoto realized the extent of Morgan's addiction, she left him. Morgan sold his trumpet and dropped out of jazz for about two years. And he lost something more valuable than his instrument—his embouchure, the practiced seal between mouth and mouthpiece.

In 1963, Morgan admitted himself to Lexington Federal Medical Prison in Kentucky to take the "Lexington Cure" and get off heroin. But at Lexington, Morgan merely picked up tips for maintaining a heroin habit, like his old boss Art Blakey, and added a little cocaine to his routine. In October 1963, he returned to New York to pick up where he left off, with music and drugs.

Within a month of returning to New York, Morgan recorded his signature album, *The Sidewinder*, which came out in July 1964. A shortened version of the title track became a surprise radio hit on the pop and R&B charts and was used in a Chrysler commercial during the 1964 World Series.

Curiously, the hit song was an afterthought. The album was short on material and the popular tale is that Morgan wrote the song within a few minutes on a roll of toilet paper, just as Dave Dictor of MDC would write "I Hate Work" on toilet paper in the bathroom of a Domino's Pizza in Austin in 1979. The success of the hit song and album surprised everyone, including Blue Note Records, which was struggling financially at the time. The album may have saved the important jazz label. Morgan earned $15,000 in royalties from *The Sidewinder*, but he spent it all on drugs.

In 1965, Morgan was so spaced out on dope that he passed out and hit his head on a hot radiator. He was so drugged up that he didn't feel the radiator scorching his scalp. When he finally came to, he had a massive, serious burn on the right side of his head. He covered it up with a bandage until his hair grew back enough to comb over the scar, resulting in some really stupid hairstyles for a few years. He stole a TV set from a hotel lobby to support his habit. And on one occasion, he arrived at Birdland in a pair of bedroom slippers, trying to play it off like that was the cool new style when the truth was that he had sold his only shoes for drugs.

By 1967, Morgan was deeply into drugs again and essentially homeless. It was only a matter of time until the talented shit show crossed paths with the Babysitter of Jazz, Helen Moore, 12 years his senior. When they finally met on a cold New York night, Morgan had no coat because he had sold it for drug money, possibly to the same guy who bought his shoes. He was missing teeth. His trumpet was in a pawn shop. Of course, Moore took him in.

"Raggedy and pitiful. For some kind of reason, my heart just went out to him," Moore said in a 1996 interview.

Moore was a great influence on Morgan. She got his trumpet out of hock and got his coat back. She fed him her good home cooking and did her best to keep him off drugs. She started representing him in the music business. Before long, Lee Morgan was back. He made several new albums.

In the summer of 1970, Morgan and his group of hot shots were invited to play a two-week engagement at the Lighthouse in Hermosa Beach, California. The Lighthouse was the top jazz club on the West Coast. Dozens of fantastic live albums have been made there. Recordings of Morgan's group from July 10, 11, and 12 were released as the double album *Live at the Lighthouse*. The album shows Morgan exploring a new style, playing looser and longer. It seemed like Morgan was about to turn a corner with his sound. And he seemed to be having a lot of fun in California. Photos from the residency show him looking lean and healthy.

Howard Rumsey, the musical director of the club from 1949 to 1971, said, "Lee lifted the band and the listeners every night with his free swinging effortless, inspiring, personal pixie-like style. He was a young man, already older than his years, thrilled with his talent and the wonders of the world around him."

Morgan, in the fever of the time, became increasingly political. He wrote a song, "Angela," in honor of political activist Angela Davis. And he was part of Rahsaan Roland Kirk's Jazz & the People's Movement, the jazz activist group that pushed for more Black music on TV.

Morgan was doing well. His records were selling. He toured across the U.S. and Europe. He'd been on television a few times. But in the early hours of New Year's Day 1972, Morgan called a friend in a panic, saying, "Something drastic is going to happen. I can feel it." By then, Moore was Morgan's common-law wife. She still handled his business affairs and domestic needs. But something was a little off. Eventually, a jazz scene gossip told her what she already suspected: Lee Morgan was having an affair.

Moore reflected, "Did I love him? Or did I think of him as my possession? And I think part of that might have been my fault because I might have started being too possessive or too much like a mother to him. I was much older than Morgan. I thought about it. Like I made him. You know. I brought you back. You belong to me. And you are not supposed to go out there and do this."

On February 19, 1972, about seven weeks after the hectic New Year's phone call, 33-year-old Morgan had a gig at a dive in New York called Slugs' Saloon, alternately reported as Slug's. The saloon was a long, narrow place, like a shoebox, with sawdust on the floors. A winter storm raged; snow and ice blanketed the city.

The friend Morgan called on New Year's was his ride to the gig. But on the way, she lost control of the wheel and totaled the car. They were shaken up, but fortunately, neither was hurt.

She tried to talk Morgan into canceling, but he didn't want to let down his audience and band. They abandoned the wreck, put on their coats, and walked the rest of the way to the club.

During a break between sets, Helen Moore showed up at the club. Unfortunately, Judith Johnson, the other woman, was there, too. Moore confronted Morgan and an argument ensued. The 46-year-old Moore hit Morgan, who pushed her back. Moore was escorted out of the club. Moments later, she reentered the club, tapped Morgan on the shoulder, and shot him, using a gun Morgan had given her for protection.

Police arrived on the scene instantly and arrested Moore. However, the poor weather delayed the ambulance for an hour. By the time it arrived, Lee Morgan was dead.

WHAT TO CHECK OUT:

Dizzy Atmosphere (1957)

Candy (1958)

The Sidewinder (1964)

Sonic Boom (1967)

Live at the Lighthouse (1970)

Parker, Charlie

August 29, 1920–March 12, 1955

MAIN INSTRUMENT: Alto saxophone, tenor saxophone

TIME IN THE SCENE: 1937–1955

GENRE: Bebop

NOTABLE QUOTABLE: "Once I could play what I heard inside me, that's when I was born."

SCENE CRED:

Like Germs singer Darby Crash, Charlie "Bird" Parker lived fast, died young, and wasn't fully understood until after he was gone. Did Charlie Parker eat at Oki-Dog like Darby? Historical records are nebulous at best, but he did drink a lot of booze and shoot a lot of heroin.

Parker was a man of incredible appetites. He'd drink full bottles of liquor by himself. He'd order 20 hamburgers and eat them all. He once refused to go onstage until he'd consumed two huge Mexican dinners. He'd take two women to bed at once. He'd practice his saxophone for long hours, to the annoyance of his neighbors.

He spent most of his short life living in ratty hotels and boarding houses as he traveled the country. When his instrument was in hock, he'd borrow one from another player or just not show up to the gig, an irksome tradition that lives on today in punk shows everywhere. He used taxi cabs as offices or for quick naps or to shoot up. His friend Robert Reisner said, "No one had such a love of life, and no one tried harder to kill himself."

"If you don't live it, it won't come out your horn," he said.

With Dizzy Gillespie and Thelonious Monk, Charlie Parker invented a new kind of music called bebop—lightning-quick, virtuosic playing with harmonies and unpredictable patterns— that was largely dismissed by critics as a fad. And bebop confused fans who wanted hummable dance music like Benny Goodman. As with anything cool, the vast majority just didn't get it. That is, if they even heard it at all. You think the Germs song "Forming" got played on the radio between "Free Bird" and "Hotel California"?

A handful of forward-thinking musicians jumped on board with bebop, but most were merely imitating the founders. Bass player Charles Mingus recognized the derivative trend and wrote the song "Gunslinging Bird," also known as "If Charlie Parker Was a Gunslinger, There'd Be a Whole Lot of Dead Copycats." You have to respect the beboppers, putting so much of themselves into their music for so little recognition. Eventually the beatniks embraced bebop as serious art made by people of integrity, but by then Parker was circling the drain.

Miles Davis, who would play with Parker before his own career skyrocketed, said, "You can tell the history of jazz in four words: Louis Armstrong. Charlie Parker."

Parker was born in 1920 in Kansas City, Kansas. When he was seven, the Parker family moved to the other Kansas City, the one in Missouri. Charles Parker Sr. was a dancer and pianist on the vaudeville circuit but eventually found more stable work with the railroad. Both jobs kept him away from home much of the time. Parker's mother, Adelaide Bailey, worked nights for Western Union. Bailey was part Black and part Choctaw. When her son was 11, Bailey bought him a new alto saxophone.

In 1934, the 14-year-old Parker joined the school band at Lincoln High School, the same school Miles Davis would attend in 1941. But within a year, Parker saw his future in music, quit school at 15, and joined the local musicians' union. He was spending all of his time at jazz clubs anyhow. He hung around them so much that someone called him a yardbird, always fluttering around the scene. Yardbird eventually became Bird, one of the most famous nicknames in music.

One event from this era has become the stuff of legend. In the spring of 1936, about a year after dropping out of school, Parker sat in with a group of older, more seasoned players at the Reno Club in Kansas City. Parker got so lost in soloing that he missed a change and screwed up the song. The cantankerous drummer pulled a cymbal off his stand and tossed it toward Parker. It landed at Parker's feet with a crash. Parker was laughed off stage. (This moment is captured strikingly in the 1988 film *Bird*, with Forest Whitaker as the young Parker.) Parker later said of the incident, "Everybody fell out laughing. I went home and cried and didn't want to play again for three months."

But when he picked the horn back up, the teenager found new fervor, sometimes toiling up to 15 hours a day. He began developing some of the ideas that would later shape bebop.

"Master your instrument. Master the music. And then forget all that bullshit and just play."

A few other milestones occurred in 1936. The 16-year-old married his high school girlfriend, Rebecca Ruffin. And he went on his first tour. On the way to a gig, Parker's ensemble was in a car accident; Parker broke three ribs and fractured his spine. The doctors prescribed strong opioid painkillers and Parker became hooked. He soon started using heroin, too. This was the beginning of Parker's lifelong struggle with substances. Parker also experienced mental illness, but whether it came before or after the substance abuse is not clear. What is clear is that the drugs and alcohol didn't help.

The next few years were a blur of practice and tours. A 1938 tour brought Parker to New York City for the first time. Kansas City was not the jazz epicenter it once was, so, in 1939, he sold his horn, bought a train ticket, abandoned his young wife, and headed to New York to be with the music. But music alone wasn't paying the bills; Parker had to wash dishes and take other part-time jobs. In New York City in 1939, Charlie Parker found the sound he was looking for.

"I kept thinking there's bound to be something else. I could hear it sometimes, but I couldn't play it."

He discovered that the 12 notes of the chromatic scale could be used as segues to any of the 24 keys. A song could change keys as many times as you wanted, whenever you wanted. These "Bird changes" freed him up to explore a wider world of sound.

Shortly after Parker's musical breakthrough, Charles Parker Sr. was stabbed to death. Parker returned to Kansas City for the funeral and squeezed in a few gigs while he was in town. At one of these gigs, he met trumpet player Dizzy Gillespie. Gillespie was already based in New York, but he never ran into Parker there. By 1941, the two of them were playing side by side in a band, jamming, and talking music on a regular basis.

They both had great ideas. Unfortunately, the Dark Age of American Music, brought on by the two-year-long musicians' strike of 1942, means that nothing the two played during this era was recorded. For two years, there were almost no new records in the U.S. And that meant the new music didn't get played on the radio, either. Bebop started out with a couple of strikes against it. The only way to hear bebop was at a club—if you were in the know.

Thelonious Monk got into the picture. Parker, Gillespie, and Monk were part of a daring, informal group that would gather late at night to explore new sounds. Monk explained, "We're going to get a big band started. We're going to create something they can't steal because they can't play it."

Older, frumpy jazz players rejected the new sounds, the inchoate bebop, but Parker, Gillespie, and Monk didn't care. They called the old farts "moldy figs," which would be a good name for a punk band.

In 1942, Parker married a second time, to Geraldine Scott, but she couldn't put up with the lack of stability that comes with having a heroin-addicted, unpopular musician for a husband, and they split up almost immediately. But it's OK. He'd have a couple more wives on the way.

By 1945, the strike was over, and people could buy new records again. Bebop started getting recorded, pressed, and distributed. Parker continued working with his cohorts Gillespie and Monk but assembled his own group. He made a record for the Savoy label, but many of his recordings from this era weren't released until after his death.

Also in 1945, Parker booked a six-week tour of California that stretched into two years. Of course, that includes a six-month stay at a mental hospital. Yeah, California wasn't a good experience for Parker. It's hard to believe, but he couldn't always find drugs there. So, he just drank more. For some reason, as the tour was winding down, Parker cashed in his bus ticket, scored some drugs, and decided to stay in Los Angeles. While there, he had some kind of freak-out in a hotel room, set his bed on fire, and ran into the lobby naked. He was sent to recover at the Camarillo State Mental Hospital, later immortalized in the Fear song "Camarillo," to get his head together.

There was a doctor at Camarillo who was a Charlie Parker fan. The doctor said Parker was "a man living from moment to moment. A man living for the pleasure principle, music, food, sex, drugs, kicks, his personality arrested at an infantile level. A man with almost no feeling of guilt and only the smallest, most atrophied nub of conscience. One of the army of psychopaths supplying the populations of prisons and mental institutions. Except for his music, a potential member of that population. But with Charlie Parker it is the music factor that makes all the difference. That's really the only reason we're interested in him. The reason we're willing to stop our own lives and clean up his messes. People like Charlie require somebody like that."[11]

After half a year, the doctors at Camarillo thought Parker was good to go and sent him on his way. Parker dried out. He was totally off drugs and alcohol and was in good spirits. Before heading back to New York, he headed into the studio to record the song "Relaxin' at Camarillo," one of my favorites.

Parker returned to New York and started what was probably his best group, the Classic Quintet, whose members included Miles Davis and Max Roach. He also immediately started using heroin again, but I think you knew that was coming.

In 1948 Parker really, really, really got off heroin, for real this time, and married his third wife, Doris Snyder. But things didn't work out and Parker—surprise—got back on heroin. At this point, you may be screaming, "What the fuck, Charlie Parker?! Are you a fucking idiot?!" It sure seems that way.

---

11 Quoted by Whitney Balliett in "Bird: The Brilliance of Charlie Parker," published in the *New Yorker* on February 23, 1976.

Parker, who had been playing music professionally for about 13 years, finally found respect when he toured Europe in 1949, where he was treated like a genius. It must have been good for his ego. Back in New York, a nightclub was named in his honor: Birdland.

> "Any musician who says he is playing better either on tea, the needle, or when he is juiced, is a plain, straight liar. When I get too much to drink, I can't even finger well, let alone play decent ideas. You can miss the most important years of your life, the years of possible creation."

In 1950, Parker took his fourth wife, Chan Berg—kinda. He just plumb forgot to divorce Doris Snyder, but since he popped out a couple of kids with Berg, the State of New York considered them a common-law couple. How many fucks did Charlie Parker give about any of this? Four out of five jazz historians say zero fucks were given. The other jazz historian couldn't be reached for comment as he was coaching his granddaughter's soccer game.

A year later, Parker was busted for heroin and lost his essential cabaret card. It was the same career groin shot that crippled Billie Holiday and Thelonious Monk. After a year, Parker's card was reinstated, but by then the clubs didn't want anything to do with the turbulent sax player. Parker retreated into the studio with Gillespie and recorded *Bird and Diz*, which was originally released as a 10-inch 78-rpm record. It documents the last time these two alchemists of bebop would share the studio.

The next few years just rolled by with Parker touring and making recordings, many of which collected dust in the vaults until after his death. Parker was drinking a lot, drugging a lot, and burning bridges. By 1954, he was banned from Birdland, the club named after him. That same year, Parker's three-year-old daughter died of pneumonia, and Parker tried to kill himself twice.

In March 1955, Parker had a gig in Boston. On his way out of town, he thought he'd pay a visit to Baroness Pannonica de Koenigswarter, the wealthy socialite who was the patron and caretaker of the unstable Thelonious Monk. Parker was one of the baroness's charity cases, too.

Parker arrived at the baroness's suite at Stanhope Hotel in New York looking and feeling like total dog shit, so she offered him an alcoholic drink, as was the style at the time. To her surprise he said no. He was fighting an ulcer and thought a glass of ice water might help. Then he started puking up blood.

The baroness summoned a doctor, who advised immediate hospitalization. But Parker refused. Against the doctor's orders and all fucking common sense, Parker got into bed in the suite. The doctor kept an eye on him over the next several days. He seemed to be improving. After a few days, he was well enough to move to the living room to watch TV. A juggling act on television made Parker laugh. Then he choked and slumped over. In a moment he was dead. It was March 12, 1955.

The baroness said, "At the moment of his going, there was a tremendous clap of thunder. I didn't think about it at the time, but I've thought about it often since; how strange it was."

The coroner said all kinds of shit was wrong with Parker, including cirrhosis, a bleeding ulcer, and lobar pneumonia, but the cause of death was a heart attack. The coroner estimated Parker's age to be between 50 and 60. He was only 34.

WHAT TO CHECK OUT:

Bird and Diz (1952)

"Bird" Symbols (1961)

Jazz 'Round Midnight (1991)

The Complete Live Performances on Savoy (1999; recorded 1947–1950)

Rich, Buddy

September 30, 1917–April 2, 1987

MAIN INSTRUMENT: Drums

TIME IN THE SCENE: 1919–1987

GENRE: Big band, bebop, hard bop

NOTABLE QUOTABLE: "I gotta go up there and be embarrassed by you motherfuckers? I played with the greatest fuckin' musicians in the world. How dare you play like that for me? You try one fuckup the next set and when you get back to New York you'll need another fuckin' job. Count on it! Now get outta my fuckin' bus."

SCENE CRED:

If you like colorful characters, profanity, and mind-blowing drum skills, Buddy Rich is, to use a Buddy Richism, your kind of person. The things this guy could do with drums and the F-word are astounding. And the Buddy Rich origin story is barely believable. Indeed, a lot of stuff about Buddy Rich defies belief.

Rich has been called the most famous drummer of the 20th century. And he often called himself the best drummer ever. He was probably right about that. He played so fast he could do drumrolls with just one hand. That particular skill came in handy, so to speak, in 1948 when he broke an arm right before a six-week tour. Rather than cancel the tour and put 19 people out of work, he played with one arm in a sling.

Rich had a bit of an ego, but he earned it. Some of the self-aggrandizing was part of the act, real old-school shtick. Rich was also known for his temper, alternately cruel and hilarious. Once, when he felt an audience in Washington, D.C., wasn't responding with enough enthusiasm, he told them he didn't need their shit, adding, "There's always Baltimore." But mostly he adored the audiences. He loved being onstage night after night. He made a ton of albums, too, which are great, but he didn't enjoy the studio.

As he put it, "No, I don't like recording. It's a bore."

Rich saved his angriest salvo for his band members. He demanded, in his own words, "one hundred and ten percent fuckin' perfection every fuckin' tune." His players took to recording his vicious harangues; the tapes have been traded hand to hand for decades. Musicians and comedians alike howl at and recoil from these candid diatribes.

"Everybody's on two weeks' notice tonight. I'm telling you, everybody gets two weeks' notice tonight. I can't handle this anymore. You're all . . . you're not my kind of people—at all. I don't understand this fuckin' kind of music at all. I don't understand what anybody is doing up there. I'm workin' my fuckin' ass off. You put that fuckin' mouthpiece into that bell again, I'm gonna take that fuckin' horn and break it across my knee! Do you understand that?"

It's funny now, but can you imagine being on that tour bus, week after week?

"If you don't enjoy it here, fuck you! And get off my band. Or we can find other ways to settle it. I'm just so fuckin' tired of having to go through speeches with you guys. You're all a fuckin' bunch of children. There's not a man among you, not one man who can go out there and play the job like a man. You're all up there, fuckin' high school, bullshit jive artists. You jived me for the last fuckin' time. You got two sets to make up your fuckin' mind or I get me an all-LA band tomorrow night. Don't think that's not impossible [sic]. It's very fuckin' possible. I've had it with you guys. I ought to give each one of you motherfuckers a cut in salary before I get out of this fuckin' room!"

Another thing about Rich is that he loved marijuana and allegedly smoked it every day. Can you imagine how intense he'd be without pot?

"I don't need this shit. I have a home in Palm Springs, and I can go sit on my ass the rest of my life and not worry about a fuckin' thing . . . and don't have to meet your fuckin' payroll and pay you for playin' like a fuckin' high school dropout! How dare you do that! ASSHOLES!"

And it goes on like that. Positively brutal. I've been trying to think of a punk rock equivalent of the explosive, explicit Buddy Rich, but nobody comes to mind.

However, I did find a former band member with nice things to say about his time with Rich. Trumpet player Ross Konikoff wrote in an online comment, "The only time I saw him as he sounds on the tapes is when he had a bad back, or a band full of young guys who couldn't play well but thought they could, who showed disrespect towards him, and thought they were too good to be there. . . . I know that tape sounds funny to most people, but to the people who knew him to be unbelievably generous, funny, loving and a whole different kind of drummer than any other on Earth, that tape hurts because we hear his pain and confusion."

Konikoff's post makes Rich all the more intriguing. He wasn't just the Tasmanian Devil of jazz. He had other factory settings besides FUCK YOU. So, where the fuck did Buddy Rich come from and how the fuck did he become the fucking legend of the fucking drums, you asshole?

Rich came from a show business family of the vaudeville era in New York City. His mother was a singer, his father a dancer. At home, his folks noticed their toddler keeping a beat on a dinner plate with a fork and knife. He was only 18 months old and could already play better than Donna Rhia, the drummer on the Germs album *Germicide*. At the theater, they noticed he kept stealing drumsticks from the band. On a lark, they put a snare drum in front of him and he could really play.

"That's going in the act," his father might have exclaimed in an old-time fashion, possibly while rubbing his hands together. And that night the child made his debut as Baby Traps, the Drum Wonder. He played "Stars and Stripes Forever" and brought down the house. It was his first addicting taste of applause. With the exception of a few breaks for medical reasons, including an operation to remove two discs from his spinal cord, Rich stayed onstage for the rest of his life.

When Rich was six and already a seasoned professional, he toured Australia for a year and a half. He officially dropped out of school in sixth grade. By the time he was 15, Rich was making $1,000 a week, a ton of money for a teenager in the middle of the Great Depression.

That made Rich the second-highest-paid child entertainer in the world, after Jackie Coogan.[12]

But things really started picking up for Rich in 1937 when the 20-year-old was picked to play in clarinetist Joe Marsala's big band. The Joe Marsala gig itself wasn't that hot, but it was a stepping stone to bigger groups, like Artie Shaw and, eventually, Tommy Dorsey. The hardworking, popular Dorsey group is where Rich met the Singing Fedora, Frank Sinatra. Two legendary hotheads in one band was too much. Rich and Sinatra exchanged blows more than once but liked and respected each other. They remained lifelong friends.

When the U.S. entered World War II, Rich enlisted in the United States Marine Corps. The USMC put him to work as a judo instructor. Yeah, somehow Rich found the time to become a black belt in judo by his early 20s. He trained the troops but never saw the battlefield.

Rich's Associated Press obituary described his time in the marines this way: "Always combative and hot-tempered, he got into numerous fights as 'the only Jew in my platoon,' he said, adding that after a dozen fights he heard no more complaints

---

12 Coogan is best known for his adult role as Uncle Fester on the *Addams Family* TV series of the 1960s. But decades earlier Coogan was the first child entertainer to earn a million dollars. Unfortunately, Coogan's parents spent all of his money, resulting in the passage of the California Child Actor's Bill, also called the Coogan Law, which requires a percentage of a child entertainer's earnings to be placed in a trust fund that becomes liquid upon legal adulthood.

about the patriotism or fighting ability of Jews." He was discharged in 1944 for a medical condition.

After being discharged, Rich rejoined the Tommy Dorsey group for a bit before realizing he wanted his own band. His old friend Frank Sinatra, the Midnight Calzone, who was a big star by this time, got Rich's first band off the ground financially. From then on, Rich was his own boss, although he'd occasionally do session work, including about half of the drums on the Charlie Parker/Dizzy Gillespie collaboration album, *Bird and Diz*, a detour from his preferred big band territory.

In 1952, jazz drummer Louie Bellson changed the look and sound of drumming forever when he invented the double bass drum kit. Rich watched this historical moment, unimpressed with Bellson but kicking himself for not thinking of it first. The next night, Rich debuted his own double bass drum act. As he later explained, "Never mind who thought of it first. I didn't play them like Louie does. He utilizes the two bass drums with his hands. I did a thing where I played a two-bass-drum solo—like dancing. I didn't use the snare drum at all. But that was only one segment of it; I played the first part of the solo on my big set. Then they rolled the two bass drums out on a platform. I came down from the big set, sat down and just played them."

This might be a good place to point out that Buddy Rich never practiced. He said he didn't have time. The only time he touched the drums was onstage or in the studio. He trained before live audiences and recording engineers.

"Almost everything I've done, I've done through my own creativity. I don't think I ever had to listen to anyone else to learn how to play drums. I wish I could say that for about 10,000 other drummers," he said.

But in 1955, Rich teamed up with one of his peers, Gene Krupa. Until Rich came along, Krupa was often cited as the best drummer alive. The studio album *Krupa and Rich* finds the two titans facing off, track by track. Krupa and Rich only appear together on one song, "Bernie's Tune," culminating in a six-minute drum battle that is still impressive. Who won the battle? That's up to the listener. But it should be noted that Gene Krupa called Rich "the greatest drummer ever to have drawn breath."

Four years later, Rich recorded a similar concept album, *Rich Versus Roach*, which found him going one-on-one with Miles Davis's hotshot drummer, Max Roach, the gentleman who punched Ornette Coleman in the mouth for playing unhinged music. Max Roach was the drummer everybody was talking about in 1959; he was great. No doubt this irked Rich, who always had to be number one. One anecdote from the time has Rich driving by Roach in a new convertible sports car with a beautiful woman in the passenger seat.

"Hey, Max! Top this!" he shouted.

The same year, Rich had his first heart attack.

Rich spent the 1950s, '60s, '70s, and '80s touring the world and doing TV shows. Live performance was his forte, recording sessions a necessary chore. He was on *The Tonight Show* with Johnny Carson several times. Carson was a close friend and a drummer, too. Rich did *The Steve Allen Show* and Lucille Ball's *Here's Lucy*. And perhaps most memorably, Episode 522 of the Muppet Show in 1981, in which Rich defeats Animal in a comedic drum battle.

Rich was a living legend. A posh jazz critic for the British newspaper the *Observer* proclaimed him "the finest drum technician, certainly in the jazz world, perhaps in all music today, possibly of all time," possibly while eating a crumpet, possibly on the Thames.

But it wasn't all Muppet drum battles and haughty proclamations. In March 1970, Rich was busted for possession of marijuana in Buffalo, New York. Oddly, the arresting officer admitted the whole thing was probably a set-up, saying, "There is a possibility that someone planted this in Mr. Rich's luggage more or less to have him arrested by devious means." The judge threw out the case. In 1974, Rich was arrested again with marijuana, this time in Tasmania. He was ordered to pay a $75 fine.

As far as drugs and arrests go, Buddy Rich was pretty low key for a jazz player. Bandmates have said his biggest addiction was junk food, which he gorged on, possibly while high.

Rich was nearly through his seventh decade in show business when disaster stuck. In March 1987, while on tour in New York, Rich was rushed to a hospital when the left side of his body became paralyzed. Doctors assumed it was from a stroke. While he rested in the New York hospital, he wondered not if he could still play the drums with half his body but if he could play drums with half his body and still be number one.

Rich was transferred to the UCLA Medical Center in Los Angeles for more tests. On March 16, 1987, doctors at UCLA discovered a brain tumor. As the medical team wheeled him into surgery, a nurse asked if there was anything he was allergic to. "Yes," he replied, "country and western music."

Rich survived the operation. But 17 days later, breathing problems and another heart attack finally silenced the Loudmouth of Jazz, the greatest drummer in the world, Bernard "Buddy" Rich.

Roach, Max

January 8, 1924–August 16, 2007

MAIN INSTRUMENT: Drums

TIME IN THE SCENE: 1944–2002

GENRE: Bebop, hard bop, modal jazz, avant-garde jazz

NOTABLE QUOTABLE: "I always resented the role of a drummer as nothing more than a subservient figure."

SCENE CRED:

I thought I was finished writing when I realized there had to be a Max Roach chapter. You may know Max Roach as "the guy who punched Ornette Coleman in the face," but there's so much more to the Max Roach story. He played with almost everyone, performed on a plethora of good records, and led his own groups. If you see his name on a record, there's a darn good chance it is darn good. And he seems to pop up in many anecdotes. That's why I like to refer to him as the Forrest Gump of Jazz. Of course, I wouldn't say that to him if he were still alive; he'd probably punch me.

I'm kidding, I'm kidding! I'm sure Max Roach didn't just go around punching people all the time. He was an articulate, educated man who only punched people for very good reasons.

Roach's birth certificate says he was born on January 10, 1924, but he's been quoted as saying the real date is January 8, 1924. In either case, he was born into poverty near something called the Great Dismal Swamp in North Carolina. Thank goodness his family found the means to move to New York City when he was four.

Roach's mother was a gospel singer, so he was always around music. She bought him a bugle. When he was about 10, he was given a snare drum and played in a marching band. When Roach was about 12, the family moved to a new apartment only to discover that the previous owner had abandoned a piano. This is where the musically precocious young man began experimenting with dynamics—hard and soft, fast and slow—and the importance of leaving space in music.

"Music mirrors where we should go, have gone and can go. Music is an abstraction."

By the early 1940s, the big band era was slowly dying; the bebop era was embryonic. For a brief moment, Roach had a foot in each era. At the age of 18, Roach was the house drummer at an important jazz club, Monroe's Uptown House. There he learned by doing, accompanying Dizzy Gillespie, Thelonious Monk, and Charlie Parker as they drafted the blueprints of bebop. Around this time, he was tapped to play with big band royalty Duke Ellington. In 1943, then 19, Roach made his first studio recording with saxophone player Coleman Hawkins, who also straddled the genres.

During this era, Roach and another drummer, Kenny Clarke, are credited with changing the sound of jazz drumming. Roach and Clarke, the theory goes, used more ride cymbals and less bass drum, setting a template for the genre. Roach in particular was known for playing fast patterns on the ride, almost like blast beats. The bass drum was reserved for dramatic accents, known in jazz as "dropping bombs." Or so goes the common perception.

But, Roach explained, "That is not what was going on. We played the bass drum, but the engineers would cover it up because it would cause distortion due to the technology at the time. There were never any mics near our feet; they would have one mic above the drum set, and that was all. . . . I've heard people say that, historically, I introduced the technique of not playing the bass drum and concentrating on the ride cymbal, which was not the case. You didn't carry a bass drum around on the subways of New York like we used to and then not use it."

Whether by intent or by the limitations of recording technology, Roach and Clarke had a sweeping effect on jazz drumming. Roach consistently tried to approach the drums as an important instrument, not just a click track for the rest of the band. As he put it, "I think that the rhythm sections, drummers in particular, are the unsung heroes of the music. It's the rhythm section that has changed the styles from one period to the other."

Roach always seemed to be in the right place at the right time. Between 1949 and 1950, he worked with the emerging Miles Davis on a series of sessions that would remain unreleased until 1957. Capitol Records hemmed and hawed over the recordings for nearly a decade because they weren't sure how to market the new music or if it was even worth releasing. When it came out in 1957 as *Birth of the Cool*, it was embraced by musicians, especially West Coast jazz guys like Dave Brubeck and Chet Baker, as the path jazz should take. The general public was a little slower to pick up on the genius of the album. Roach played on 7 of the 11 songs. Today it is considered one of the most important recordings of the 20th century. In 1959, the Davis/Roach lightning would strike again on *Kind of Blue*, which is not a bad thing to have on your drumming resume.

In 1950, Roach went to college, studying classical percussion at the Manhattan School of Music. He earned his bachelor of music degree in 1953 and continued studying and teaching music for almost five decades. While he was working on his degree, he was playing and recording with Miles Davis, Chet Baker, Charles Mingus, Charlie Parker, Thelonious Monk, Duke Ellington, Dizzy Gillespie, Bud Powell, and more. A quick glance at jazzdisco.org shows Roach worked 50 studio sessions during his three years in music school. I have to wonder if Max Roach drank a lot of black coffee.

In 1952, when he was still in college, Roach and bassist Charles Mingus started their own record label, Debut Records, to have total creative control of their music and to help developing artists who might not find a record label elsewhere, sort of like what I did from 1991 to 2008 with my own label, Burrito Records. Debut Records released titles by Bud Powell, Teo Macero, Oscar Pettiford, Eric Dolphy, and others, while I released records by Flaming Midget, Scrotum Grinder, Gay Cowboys in Bondage, and Sodomized By Marcia Brady.

Shortly after finishing college, on May 15, 1953, Roach joined living legends Charlie Parker, Dizzy Gillespie, Charles Mingus, and Bud Powell for a gig in Toronto. Tapes were rolling that night. The recordings became the album *Jazz at Massey Hall* on Debut Records. Jazz fans sometimes call this live recording "the greatest concert ever." Or at least that is how Mingus and Roach marketed it. Hyperbole or not, it's a good record and historically important. And once again, Roach totally Gumped to the occasion.

One of the bright spots of *Jazz at Massey Hall* is "Drum Conversation," a four-minute solo, in which Roach shows that the drums can be a lead instrument. These four minutes would go on to influence future generations of rock drummers like John Bonham and Ginger Baker. Nearly three decades later, in an interview with Scott K. Fish, then the managing editor of *Modern Drummer*, Roach would talk about the drum as a lead instrument and the process of creating a drum solo: "What makes a piece an art piece is design. . . . Like creating a poem, a painting, or anything else. It's how you . . . set up certain things. . . . Space is important, and dynamics are important. And things like sequences. . . . And how you relate to certain timbres on the set itself is important. And that's how you build a solo."

Roach continued drumming and pursued teaching. He became a professor at the Lenox School of Jazz in Massachusetts. In 1972, the eloquent and erudite Roach joined the faculty of the University of Massachusetts Amherst, where he taught music until the mid-1990s.

By the late 1950s, perhaps inspired by his label partner and sometimes-bandmate, the outspoken bassist Charles Mingus, Roach had also become politically engaged. In July 1960, Roach and Mingus protested the Newport Jazz Festival when they learned Black artists were being paid less than white artists.

And Roach's defining piece of protest jazz was the 1960 album *We Insist! Max Roach's Freedom Now Suite*. The album consisted of five exploratory compositions, including vocals by Abbey Lincoln, all pertaining to the civil rights movement. Roach and Lincoln married a couple of years later.

Roach later said of this time, "That was a period of total protest, and I was heavily involved in the civil rights movement. I've never believed in art just for the sake of art. It is entertainment, of course, and dancing is also part of it, but it can also be for enlightenment." I believe Crass, Discharge, Dead Kennedys, and MDC would applaud this statement.

Roach recorded about nine albums as a bandleader in the 1960s and played as a sideman on many more.

"I will never again play anything that does not have social significance. We American jazz musicians of African descent have proved beyond all doubt that we are master musicians of our instruments. Now what we have to do is employ our skill to tell the dramatic story of our people and what we've been through. . . . My point is that we must decolonize our minds and rename and redefine ourselves. . . . In all respects, culturally, politically, socially, we must redefine ourselves and our lives, in our own terms."

The 1970s found Roach balancing music and a teaching career. He formed a group called M'Boom, which he referred to as a percussion orchestra. This large ensemble used all sorts of percussion instruments to create a unique sound, proving that not all drummers are just noise-banging idiots with herpes.

Never one to rest, Roach wrote music for theater in the 1980s. He also became an early supporter of rap music, saying of rappers, "They had all this talent, and they had no instruments. So, they started rap music. They rhymed on their own. They made their own sounds and their own movements." In 1983, he performed with two DJs and a crew of break dancers.

In the 1990s, Roach's teaching and touring slowed down a little, and by 2002 he'd retired from both. With 58 years in music and about 45 years in music education, he'd touched a lot of lives. His fingerprints are all over jazz history. Around this time, he was diagnosed with hydrocephalus, a buildup of fluid in the brain. Roach died on August 16, 2007, from Alzheimer's. Nearly 2,000 people attended his funeral.

I don't know if there is a Jazz Heaven. But if there is, you can be sure Max Roach is there right now, punching Ornette Coleman in the face.

WHAT TO CHECK OUT:

The Max Roach Quartet Featuring Hank Mobley (1953)

Max Roach + 4 (1956)

MAX (1958)

We Insist! Max Roach's Freedom Now Suite (1960)

Percussion Bitter Sweet (1961)

Drums Unlimited (1966)

Rollins, Sonny

September 7, 1930–STILL ALIVE

MAIN INSTRUMENT: Tenor saxophone

TIME IN THE SCENE: 1947–2014

GENRE: Hard bop, bebop

NOTABLE QUOTABLE: "I feel that I have an obligation to jazz and also to myself to play as good as I can play."

SCENE CRED:

Whenever I hear people say, "Ugh! I hate Rollins! He sucks," I say, "Well, have you heard *Saxophone Colossus*?" And then they say, "Are you a cop or something?" For the record (ahem), I am not a cop and I like both Rollinses. The good news is both Rollinses are still alive at the time of this writing. And Sonny Rollins seems like one of the coolest dudes in jazz, the one I'd like to have a long lunch with and just talk to.

A legitimate living legend and one of the last O.G. jazz cats standing, Rollins has rightfully been honored with a GRAMMY Lifetime Achievement Award, the National Medal of Arts, honorary doctorates from 10 colleges and universities, and several other titles and acknowledgements. Yet he seems humble and reserved, with nothing to prove anymore.

"I'm fortunate that I'm making a living at it now because I'm not equipped to do anything else."

Theodore Rollins was born in Harlem in 1930, in the middle of the Great Depression, right at the start of swing, not far from the heralded Apollo Theatre. He grew up just doors from his saxophone idol, Coleman Hawkins. Of course, he was destined to be a musician.

Rollins started out on piano but switched to saxophone when he was seven or eight. Growing up in the Fourth Cradle of Jazz put Rollins in close proximity to Charlie Parker, Miles Davis, Bud Powell, and others. Although Rollins is mostly self-taught, pianist Thelonious Monk became his mentor. By the time he was 18, he was a professional. By the time he was 19, he was playing on recordings with Art Blakey, Bud Powell, J.J. Johnson, and more. He's expressed gratitude for experiences like these: "I've played with all of the heavyweights in the modern jazz, progressive jazz movement. I've been fortunate enough to play with them, a who's who. All of those guys, I've been fortunate enough to have performed with."

His parents had come to New York from the Virgin Islands. The flavor of the Caribbean would seep into his music, giving him a sound like no other. But his foundation was the peppy bebop of Charlie Parker, Dizzy Gillespie, and Thelonious Monk. Rollins soon became known for his improvisational skills, his soloing that was spontaneous but technically proficient and in control. In the late 1950s he began experimenting with unaccompanied solos, something he would continue to do for the rest of his career.

"I feel that jazz improvisation is the ultimate. You have to create on the spot, the essence of this music."

His close working relationships with the giants of jazz were an education but also a hazard. He was addicted to heroin before he was 20. In 1950, Rollins resorted to robbery to finance his drug habit, got caught, and was sent to Rikers Island for 10 months. After his time in Riker's, Rollins squeezed in gigs with Charlie Parker, Thelonious Monk, and Miles Davis until he was caught again with heroin and returned to prison for violating parole.

Upon his second release, Rollins got to work writing. During this time, he produced some of his best-known compositions, like "Oleo," "St. Thomas," and "Doxy," which would become jazz standards, covered over and over. But he was still messing around with heroin. In 1955, Rollins entered the Jazz Junkie Hall of Shame, the Lexington Federal Medical Prison, joining the ranks of troubled jazz talents—like Chet Baker, Lee Morgan, and Sonny Stitt—who spent time in that facility. There he volunteered for a then-experimental methadone therapy. The new procedure worked. Upon release from Lexington, Rollins moved to Chicago, away from the bad influences and temptations of New York, to transition back into music. Rollins was afraid that without heroin he wouldn't be able to play as well. But he soon found himself playing better than before; his career escalated.

Clean of drugs and with his musical chops back in shape, Rollins returned to New York in 1956 and started cranking out solo albums, one classic after another, like *Tenor Madness*, *Sonny Rollins Plus 4*, and the gem of this era, *Saxophone Colossus*.

"I'm not supposed to be playing, the music is supposed to be playing me. I'm just supposed to be standing there with the horn, moving my fingers. The music is supposed to be coming through me; that's when it's really happening," he said.

Within a year, he played on the upbeat and stylish Miles Davis album *Bags' Groove* and toured in California, where he met the unconventional saxophone player Ornette Coleman.

Rollins and Coleman jammed together, and a bit of Coleman's frenzied, uninhibited style rubbed off on him. The Coleman influence can be heard on the 1958 album *Freedom Suite*. The title track is 19 minutes of blues-based spontaneity. This was also the time when Rollins started being more vocal about civil rights. In the album's liner notes, he wrote, "How ironic that the Negro, who more than any other people, can claim America's culture as his own, is being persecuted and repressed; that the Negro, who has exemplified the humanities in his very existence, is being rewarded with inhumanity."

In 1959, Rollins made his first tour of Europe, playing Germany, Italy, Sweden, the Netherlands, and France. He discovered what earlier jazz pioneers already knew: the Continent offered better money and more respect.

"Jazz has an audience all around the globe and has had for many decades," he said. "I think speaking of the United States, let's say that what we need is more of an official recognition. . . . I think what we need is a more welcoming mode from the people who put on a hundred million country-western shows on television. How about a monthly jazz show?"

Even though his playing was excellent, even though he was working steadily, even though he was adored by critics, fans, and fellow jazz artists, Rollins felt he was at a creative plateau. In 1959, he stepped out of the public eye for a while, taking a two-year sabbatical to concentrate on his health and to search for a creative breakthrough in private. As he explained, "I was getting very famous at the time, and I felt I needed to brush up on various aspects of my craft. I felt I was getting too much, too soon, so I said, wait a minute, I'm going to do it my way. I wasn't going to let people push me out there, so I could fall down. I wanted to get myself together, on my own."

He worked on his physical fitness and diet. He started studying yoga. And he spent about two years practicing his saxophone, up to 16 hours a day. Rollins didn't want his ceaseless saxophone practice to disturb a pregnant neighbor, so he took his rehearsals outside, to the Williamsburg Bridge, where he jammed every day from 1959 to 1961, looking for his next artistic peak. In the summer of 1961, a writer for a jazz magazine recognized Rollins on the bridge and asked him what the hell he was doing. The ensuing article in *Metronome* whetted the public's appetite for new Rollins records. But he wasn't ready yet. In November, Rollins returned to the public with an anticipated residency at the Jazz Gallery in Greenwich Village. Then he returned to the studio and recorded *The Bridge*, released in April 1962. The album, probably his best, became one of his bestsellers. In 2015, *The Bridge* was inducted into the GRAMMY Hall of Fame.

More albums and touring followed. He toured Japan for the first time in 1963. He was on a hot streak when he decided he needed another break to get his head together.

From 1966 to 1971, Rollins focused on yoga, mental health, and spirituality. He studied Eastern religion, including Buddhism. He visited India, Japan, and Jamaica. The Zen jazz master said, "The jazz music business is always bad. It's never good. So that led me to stop playing in public for a while again. During the second sabbatical, I worked in Japan a little bit, and went to India after that and spent a lot of time in a monastery. . . . I took some time off to get myself together and I think it's a good thing for anybody to do."

Rested and ready, Rollins returned to live music in 1971 and the recording studio in 1972. Like all forward-thinking jazz artists in the 1970s, Rollins sought to break new ground. He added electric guitar, electric bass, and even a bagpipes player. He incorporated funk elements into his compositions. His solos got longer.

President Jimmy Carter invited Rollins and his group, the Milestone Jazzstars, to play on the South Lawn of the White

House. Carter had good taste in music—or at least curiosity. He added albums by the Clash, the Sex Pistols, and the Ramones to the official White House record collection, but his successor, the evil Ronald Reagan, banished the vinyl to the White House basement.[13]

By the 1980s, Rollins had the luxury of becoming pickier with his bookings. He stopped playing tiny nightclubs and concentrated on concert halls and outdoor venues. It was a brilliant business strategy; his booking fee increased. But it was also for his own well-being.

In 1981, the Rolling Stones were in New York, working on the *Tattoo You* album. They decided a few songs could use some saxophone. Charlie Watts, the only jazz guy in the band, suggested Sonny Rollins. None of the other Stones knew who he was, but calls were made, and Rollins showed up to the session. He recorded three songs, including "Waiting on a Friend." The band was thrilled with the solos. Bumbling and oblivious, Keith Richards told Rollins to keep it up, that he might have a future in the music business. Rollins is uncredited on the album.

There were fewer albums in the 1980s, 1990s, and 2000s, but Rollins continued to tour on his deserved reputation. South America, Europe, Australia, Asia—he conquered much of the world. In 2012 Rollins played his last concert, and in 2014 he officially retired from music due to poor health. He was diagnosed with pulmonary fibrosis, a form of lung disease.

---

13 On November 22, 1977, a varied group of scientists and engineers were at the White House. President Carter asked each one about their fields of work and their accomplishments. Adorably, when Carter learned that one of the visitors was Peter Carl Goldmark, the CBS engineer who invented the LP, the leader of the free world diverged from his scripted remarks and fawned all over Goldmark, saying he was particularly grateful for innovation. Sadly, Goldmark died just 15 days later.

"I love music of course, but I don't listen anymore. . . . It's too frustrating to listen to music when I can't participate. . . . Jazz never ends . . . it just continues."

WHAT TO CHECK OUT:

Moving Out (1956)

Tenor Madness (1956)

Saxophone Colossus (1957)

Freedom Suite (1958)

Newk's Time (1959)

The Bridge (1962)

Sonny Meets Hawk! (1963)

Seconds, Kevin

March 24, 1961–STILL ALIVE

MAIN INSTRUMENT: Vocals, guitar

TIME IN THE SCENE: 1979–present

GENRE: Punk, hardcore

NOTABLE QUOTABLE: "TV sports, they all suck shit! Yeah, Howard Cosell is a wimp!"

SCENE CRED:

Although technically not a jazz artist at all, Kevin Seconds has written more songs than Duke Ellington and Adam Sandler combined and is therefore pretty neat. He's probably writing a song *right now*. And of course, everyone is familiar with the Kevin Seconds Theorem, which can be expressed as $KS > DE + AS$.

WHAT TO CHECK OUT:

Skins, Brains & Guts (1982)

Committed for Life (1983)

The Crew (1984)

Blasts from the Past (1985)

Walk Together, Rock Together (1985)

Sun Ra

May 22, 1914–May 30, 1993

MAIN INSTRUMENT: Piano, keyboards

TIME IN THE SCENE: 1934–1992

GENRE: Big band, cool jazz, avant-garde jazz, experimental

NOTABLE QUOTABLE: "Those who will not dance will have to be shot."

SCENE CRED:

The Sun Ra discography is vast, one of the largest bodies of work in jazz. There isn't even an exact count of how many records he's made, but the general consensus is more than 100 albums and dozens of singles. I've only heard a sliver of his output thus far; there's still a lot for me to discover.

Like the early 1980s Yugoslavian hardcore band Herpes Distress, Sun Ra is one of those secret-handshake artists; when you meet someone else who knows Sun Ra, you know you're on the same team. Curiously for such a prolific artist, his records are hard to find in physical format. Some of the earliest Sun Ra titles were produced by his own label in quantities as small as 75 copies—with covers hand drawn by members of the group—and sold only at concerts several decades ago. You'd have better luck finding copies of the two original Eat records, *Communist Radio* and *God Punishes the Eat*. And talk about a weird guy!

"Let me write my music not for Earth alone but for the worlds."

I had a chance to see Sun Ra in the late 1980s, but I didn't go. I had no idea who he was. And when my friends who did know tried to describe the music, it did not compute. Compared to my beloved Ramones with their matching jackets, predictable structures, barre chords, and catchy choruses, Sun Ra sounded like he was from outer space. Actually, that's what he told people.

Sun Ra was born Herman Poole Blount in Birmingham, Alabama, in 1914, but he told people he was from Saturn. He had some far-out ideas that incorporated Egyptian mythology, science fiction, Freemasonry, numerology, Kabbalah, *The Tibetan Book of the Dead*, and other arcane sources. But he didn't call his ideas a philosophy. He didn't like that word. He called his beliefs an equation. There are those who say that the Sun Ra equation was just part of the act. Some say he was nuts. Others have gone as far as calling him a fraud. Even today, some traditional jazz snobs get offended at the mere mention of his name, huffing, "That's not jazz!" So he definitely did something right. Me, I just dig the music.

The Sun Ra story is confusing and convoluted by design. Throughout his life, he evaded questions about his origins, claiming to be a visitor from the stars, bringing a message of peace through music. He used many different names and routinely denied his birth name. Much of what is known about the mysterious Alabamian from Saturn, including his date of birth, was only uncovered as recently as 1998 in the book *Space Is the Place: The Lives and Times of Sun Ra* by noted jazz writer John Szwed, who had to dig deep for the data.

"I have many names; some call me Mr. Ra, others call me Mr. Re. You can call me Mr. Mystery," he said, which didn't help clear anything up.

When he was still Herman Blount from Alabama, he began playing piano as a child. In the home, he was called Sonny. By the time he was 11, he could sight-read music and compose songs.

Birmingham was a frequent tour stop on the jazz circuit, so as a teenager, he went to see big bands. He memorized the songs as he heard them and transcribed the music to paper when he got home. Maybe he *was* from outer space.

He was a musical sponge. As he grew musically, his style incorporated blues, classical music, stride piano, Dixieland, and bebop. His influences ranged from Fats Waller to Chopin to Thelonious Monk. By the time he was a teenager, music was his life. He was an honor roll student, quiet and bookish, with few close friends if any. He lived a life of celibacy, possibly because he suffered from cryptorchidism, meaning his testicles never dropped. They remained impacted and were a source of pain for his entire life. He found comfort and fulfillment through music.

Blount played in all sorts of bands, learning many styles and how to improvise. He also turned to reading. There was a Black Masonic temple in Birmingham with an impressive library. There he explored ancient texts that would become part of the Sun Ra equation.

He was 20 when he landed his first professional job in music. His former high school biology teacher who wanted to be a singer put together a band, including Blount on piano. He joined the musicians' union, and they toured the Southeast and the Midwest in 1934. But the biology teacher/singer realized she needed to move to New York to make it in the music business. She took off for the city and left the band to Blount. He renamed the group the Sonny Blount Orchestra. But it was hard to keep a large jazz band on stable financial ground in Depression-era Alabama, and the group split up after four or five months. Sonny, as he was known professionally by then, continued playing all over town whenever there was an opportunity. At this time, his music was largely in the big band style, which was popular at the time.

When Blount was 22, he won a scholarship to Alabama Agricultural and Mechanical University, now known as Alabama A&M, to study music. But he dropped out after a year. The dropout story is one of many discrepancies in the life of Blount/Sun Ra. He claims to have dropped out of college in 1936 or 1937 because he had a cosmic vision: "My whole body changed into something else. I could see through myself. And I went up. . . . I wasn't in human form. . . . I landed on a planet that I identified as Saturn. . . . They teleported me and I was down onstage with them. They wanted to talk with me. They had one little antenna on each ear. A little antenna over each eye. They talked to me. They told me to stop [college] because there was going to be great trouble in schools. . . . The world was going into complete chaos. . . . I would speak and the world would listen. That's what they told me."

This seems like a good place to point out that Blount/Sun Ra abstained from drugs and alcohol his entire life. And the date of the alleged cosmic vision has been called into question by people who worked closely with him, saying that it occurred in Chicago in 1952. Furthermore, there are those who say that it never happened at all; that it was all part of a constructed persona that he began assembling in the early 1950s. Another possibility is that he was mentally ill.

In 1942, Blount received a draft notice. He refused to fight, calling himself a conscientious objector. He told the all-white draft board he was religiously and morally opposed to war. He told them he had to take care of family. He even showed them his empty ball sack, for fuck's sake, but the draft board would not dismiss him.

Undaunted, he filed an appeal and won. Blount would be allowed to serve his country by doing civil service work in

Pennsylvania, a much more desirable assignment than getting shot at by Nazis. But he did not turn up for service. The authorities easily caught up with him in Birmingham; he was arrested and charged with a felony. In court, Blount flat-out told the judge that if the army gave him a gun he would shoot the first high-ranking officer he saw. The judge didn't like that kind of talk at all. He called the defendant the N-word and sent him to jail.

Obviously a young, strange character like Blount was not going to do well behind bars. He sent a letter to the United States Marshals Service, writing that he was suicidal and on the verge of a nervous breakdown. After about two months behind bars, he was granted conscientious objector status and sent to Pennsylvania to do forestry work, the same sweet deal that he'd gotten himself into so much trouble by dodging. A government psychiatrist at the work camp labeled Blount "a psychopathic personality. . . sexually perverted." A month later, the government finally acknowledged Blount's undescended testicles as a legitimate medical concern and let him return to Alabama, where he went back to making music.

By 1945, Blount realized he had nothing keeping him in Alabama. He could move anywhere he wanted. By this time, Chicago, the Third Cradle of Jazz, had lost a lot of musicians to New York City. New York was the obvious choice, but Blount chose Chicago, the shrinking scene. Maybe he lacked the confidence to try New York. Maybe he didn't know that Chicago was drying up. Maybe he preferred Chicago-style pizza. Whatever the reason, Blount thrived in the Windy City.

He quickly fell in with blues singer Wynonie Harris and entered a recording studio for the first time at 32 years old, a late start in the jazz world. He also found work playing live with saxophone player Coleman Hawkins, who was at his peak, and pianist Fletcher Henderson, whose career was in decline. After seven years of being a professional sideman in the Chicago music scene, Blount started his own group, the Space Trio.

The name was some indication of the direction that would transform Herman Poole Blount from Alabama into Sun Ra from Saturn. Blount added musicians to the group. The Space Trio was no longer a trio. It became the Arkestra, and Blount began writing more complicated songs. Jazz historians call this time his cosmic jazz era. The music of the cosmic jazz era is well played, well recorded, and his most accessible, not too weird yet.

On October 20, 1952, he legally changed his name to Le Sony'r Ra and rejected the name Blount as a slave name. He used both Le Sony'r Ra and Sun Ra interchangeably for a short time before settling on the famous moniker, in homage to the ancient Egyptian sun king. But around this time, something important happened that helped that moniker to become famous.

Sun Ra, who was in his late 30s, met Alton Abraham, a smart 18-year-old jazz fan. Abraham was motivated and organized. And quite frankly, Sun Ra could barely find his ass with both hands. Abraham became Sun Ra's business manager, personal assistant, and confidant. The teenager booked concerts, scheduled practices, found new musicians to audition, and handled the money. Without Abraham, the Sun Ra story might have fizzled out in early 1950s Chicago.

The odd couple became best friends and business partners. They bounced quirky ideas off of each other. Adorably, they started a little book club in the jazz scene to exchange knowledge and opinions. The book club printed flyers and pamphlets with their unusual theories and distributed them around town, a foreshadowing of punk rock zine culture. The twosome took what they learned printing and distributing pamphlets and started their own record label, usually called El Saturn Records. But because this is Sun Ra we're talking about, sometimes the label was known as El Saturn Research, Satur Records, or just Saturn. The label released nearly 200 titles, mostly by the Sun Ra Arkestra but also by a few affiliated musicians. Amazingly, El Saturn Records survives to this day, run by a relative of Abraham.

By the late 1950s, the Arkestra was wearing wild, homemade costumes incorporating bits of science fiction, Egyptian mythology, and whatever other cosmic scraps they could grab. Nobody else was doing anything like this, and no one would until Funkadelic a decade later. Predictably, the outlandish stage garb drew detractors and supporters, sort of like the Sex Pistols in 1976. Naturally, Sun Ra loved any kind of reaction. He thought jazz was a stuffy scene that could use a dose of comedy and a flash of color. And the Arkestra grew to 20 or 30 people. The band was a revolving cast, with some members playing for years and others seemingly at random. Sort of like Kathleen Lynch, the sometimes go go dancer of the Butthole Surfers who would appear onstage when she felt like it. In fact, the Arkestra had their own dancers. They even had a fire breather, just to keep things interesting. And this was before Jerry A. of Poison Idea was even born. Scores of people passed through the Arkestra. Perhaps four score and seven, possibly a hundred or more.

Some of the albums released during this era include *Jazz by Sun Ra*, *Jazz in Silhouette*, *Sun Ra Visits Planet Earth*, *Super-Sonic Jazz*, and *We Travel the Space Ways*.

"The possible has been tried and failed. Now it's time to try the impossible."

By the end of 1961, Sun Ra and Abraham realized they should take the group and their record label to New York City. In New

York, the entire Arkestra lived in a communal house. As head of the band and head of the household, Sun Ra called band practice whenever he fucking felt like it. Artistically, the New York era is when the Sun Ra Arkestra really took off. More members were added, including multiple percussionists. Electronic instruments, like the electric piano and synthesizers, which the group had started using sparingly as early as 1956, became more prominent. They also started experimenting with tape loops and primitive delay effects. Around this time, Sun Ra was saddled with the "avant-garde jazz" tag, but it was a label he didn't particularly like. Avant-garde jazz or free jazz is almost completely made up on the spot, live or in the studio. Sun Ra insisted his music was carefully planned, saying, "I have to make sure that every note, every nuance, is correct."

In the spring of 1966, the Arkestra scored a residency, playing every Monday night at Slugs' Saloon, the same shoebox-shaped nightclub where Lee Morgan was murdered six years later. At Slugs', the band was embraced by the strangest people in the city. Even Dizzy Gillespie and Thelonious Monk checked them out and cheered them on. The Arkestra played Slugs' every Monday for a year and a half. But New York was too expensive, even with Abraham's careful money handling. In 1968, the whole organization moved to Philadelphia.

The band found a place on Morton Street, which would remain Sun Ra's home base for the rest of his career. Philadelphia was a good fit for the Arkestra. Even though they could get a little loud now and then, their neighbors liked them. They played free concerts all over the city. And Sun Ra became a local legend with his frequent guest appearances on WXPN radio. In 1968, the 54-year-old took his 30-piece band on their first tour. The psychedelic era was in full swing, and they played with the

Grateful Dead. The Dead probably loved the show, but the hippy audience was mostly confused.

Even though Sun Ra had been playing music for more than three decades, he was still almost completely unknown until *Rolling Stone* put him on the cover of its April 19, 1969, issue, bringing his name and face to millions. Also in 1969, the Arkestra released *Atlantis*, the first Sun Ra record to reach my ears and the one I turn to most often. The quirky, low-fi beeps and boops of *Atlantis* are the ice bridge between jazz and the likes of Devo, Futurisk, Count Vertigo, and K.T.H.[14]

In 1970, while Ronald fucking Reagan was still the governor of California, Sun Ra toured internationally for the first time. He

---

14 What, you don't know K.T.H.? That's understandable. Permit me this three-paragraph detour to tell you the tale of K.T.H., as it is one of the best stories in punk. In 1980, a couple of friends in Miami were at a flea market looking at junk. At one table, they found a cardboard box of crap marked "25 cents," so they started digging. One of them found a business-sized envelope. Inside was a gift certificate for eight hours of studio time at Criteria Studios, one of the best recording facilities in the world. Artists like James Brown, Aretha Franklin, Eric Clapton, the Allman Brothers, Grand Funk Railroad, the Eagles, the Bee Gees, Bob Seger, Ted Nugent, Lynyrd Skynyrd, and AC/DC made albums there.

The guy who found the envelope asked the guy at the flea market table, "Uh, how much is this old envelope?" The guy at the table said, "Everything in that box is a quarter." They plunked down a quarter and started a band.

Specifically, they started the band in the studio. They called a couple of friends and told them to go to Criteria—and bring a fucking saxophone. The people at the world-class studio were not pleased that they had to record a bunch of dudes fucking around in their fancy studio for free—what if ABBA needed the studio?—but they honored the gift certificate. From what I was told by the drummer, they spent every bit of their eight hours cutting five bizarre jams. They released two of the songs, "Skull Bossing" and "Mutant," as a 7-inch record. Just 300 copies were made—200 of them with the labels on the wrong sides! The band decorated the plain white covers by hand, no two alike. I'm sure Sun Ra would have loved this story. With the intention of naming their band something more offensive than Dead Kennedys, they called the project K.T.H., which stood for Kill The Hostages, the opposite of an homage to the 52 Americans then being held in the Iranian hostage crisis. The crisis was the final nail in the coffin of the Carter presidency and the open door to the Ronald Reagan presidency. I don't know if Sun Ra voted in 1980—or ever—but I bet he wouldn't have voted for fucking Reagan.

played the UK, France, and Germany. People in Europe already knew his music and they embraced the live experience. As usual with jazz, Europe got it more than America. As Sun Ra said, "All these other nations seem to appreciate what I'm doing, and they want me to play the furthest-out things."

In 1971, Sun Ra finally got to see Egypt with his band. The Arkestra returned in 1983 and 1984. Some of these concerts were recorded and released as albums. Also in 1971, Sun Ra was appointed artist-in-residence at the University of California, Berkeley. And he was permitted to teach a class he called The Black Man in the Cosmos, which was part talk, part jam session. Hardly anyone signed up for the class, but a lot of random people just popped in for the experience.

"I use music as a medium to talk to people," he said.

On January 30, 1975, the Sun Ra Arkestra played a concert in Cleveland. The opening act was an inchoate version of Devo. The Sun Ra performance was recorded and released as *Live in Cleveland*. I wonder if anybody bothered to record baby Devo.

A few years later, Sun Ra and Arkestra member Bill Sebastian worked together to build something they called, gloriously, the Outer Space Visual Communicator, or OVC. The OVC was a complex lighting system, constructed like an organ, that could be operated with keys and foot switches to create far-out, spacey imagery. They put it in the act.

The Arkestra and its ever-changing cast of misfits continued playing for almost two more decades. In 1990, the 76-year-old Sun Ra had a stroke, which slowed down his tour schedule. On July 4, 1992, Sun Ra played at New York's Central Park with Sonic Youth, who probably loved every minute of the madness. But his health continued to decline. By 1992, the space man who traveled the world with his message of peace could no longer play. He returned to Birmingham, where his oldest sister, Mary, became his caretaker. His heart was weakened, and his breathing was labored. He suffered more strokes. He died on May 30, 1993, with 79 trips around the sun and more than 1,000 songs to his name.

WHAT TO CHECK OUT:

Jazz in Silhouette (1959)

The Futuristic Sounds of Sun Ra (1962)

The Heliocentric Worlds of Sun Ra Vols. 1–2 (1965)

Atlantis (1969)

Space Is the Place (1973)

Young, Lester

August 27, 1909–March 15, 1959

MAIN INSTRUMENT: Tenor saxophone

TIME IN THE SCENE: 1933–1959

GENRE: Big band, swing

NOTABLE QUOTABLE: "Show them that you're an individual."

SCENE CRED:

If you still don't think jazz is cool, check out Lester Young, who literally coined the word "cool" as we use it today. Young was a soft-spoken man, but he had a way with words. He also came up with "threads" for clothing and "dig" for understand. And he was the first to call money "bread."

"How does the bread smell?" was his way of asking how much a job paid, an expression I think we should strive to bring back. Another Youngism that didn't catch on—but should have—is referring to a sick person as "Johnny Deathbed." And he called his on-again-off-again boss, Count Basie, his "homeboy" way before the Fresh Prince was even born and raised in West Philadelphia.

Young also liked to look good. He dressed neatly and took care of his hygiene. Once Young asked one of his three non-concurrent wives to sketch an idea on a piece of paper. Then he rushed the drawing to a haberdasher and asked him to bring the idea to life. The result was the porkpie hat, which became one of his trademarks. (A few months after Young's death, bassist Charles Mingus wrote and recorded the send-off "Goodbye Pork Pie Hat.")

Young gave his friend and sometime musical collaborator Billie Holiday the title "Lady Day." Holiday called him "Prez," short for President, because he always looked classy. Of course, in the boys' club world of jazz, some people thought that Young's fastidious appearance and soft manners meant he was gay. His hair was too long, his voice was too quiet, and his hand gestures were too effeminate. Some of the musicians in the Count Basie band called him "Miss Thing." But Young wasn't gay and he gave the bullies some attitude right back, calling his bandmates "ladies," which was considered a sick burn back then. Lester Young was by all accounts a shy, sweet, kind, vulnerable man, and some people just didn't understand that in his day.

"The critics used to call me the honk man. Mike Levin said I had a cardboard sound and that I couldn't play my horn. You dig? That made it harder to play my horn. That's why I don't put the kids down," he recalled.

Young had a unique way of playing the saxophone, too. Instead of holding it in front of his body, he played it to the side, like a flute. His style on the horn was as sweet as his demeanor. He liked to play slowly and softly without using too many notes. He was an acclaimed improvisor. However, for most of Young's career, he was relegated to the role of sideman in orchestras. He worked several times each with the regal Count Basie and his best friend Billie Holiday. But just because he was in the background didn't mean his work went unnoticed. Upstart musicians picked up on Young's relaxed, melodic style and used bits of it to form the cool-jazz style. By the time Young started leading his own bands and making records with his name on the cover, he was in the decade of his death.

Young's family was from New Orleans, but his mother traveled to the small town of Woodville, Mississippi, during her pregnancy and gave birth to him there on August 27, 1909. Then it was back to New Orleans.

Jazz had been born in New Orleans about a decade earlier, but it was just getting off the ground. Although the 78-rpm record was invented in 1898, there weren't even any jazz records yet. Young was eight when the first jazz record was released in 1917. Willis Handy Young, Lester's father, was an excellent musician. The whole family learned from him. Young studied trumpet, violin, and drums when he was just a child.

Young's parents split up in 1919. The dad took the three kids, and, like any good father would do in 1919, joined the fucking circus and started a band. Willis Handy Young called his child labor ensemble the Young Family Band and dragged them around the country for eight years. It was like the Partridge Family but without the Mondrian school bus and with more head lice. During the circus years, Lester switched from drums to saxophone. This is also when Lester started creating his unique personal lexicon. He and his dad—surprise—didn't get along. In late 1927 or early 1928, he quit the forced-labor circus band in Salina, Kansas, and looked for work in music. He was 18 and free.

It was a good time and place to quit. Jazz moved from New Orleans to Kansas City, Missouri, in the 1920s, and it wasn't hard for Young to get there and find opportunities. Performing with various groups, he zig-zagged around the country: Phoenix, Oklahoma City, Minneapolis. He played with Count Basie off and on from 1933 to 1949. Young was an odd person, so perhaps it is appropriate that one of his firings from the Basie group happened for an odd reason. On December 13, 1940, the superstitious Lester Young refused to take the stage because it was Friday the 13th, and he was dismissed. Or so goes the legend.

Another Young legend involves the Fletcher Henderson Orchestra. Henderson's star saxophone player, Coleman Hawkins, couldn't make a show, so Young was called in as a replacement. The two saxophone players had very different styles. He was happy to replace Hawkins, but he wasn't interested in imitating him. He played his own way and got the boot. He headed back to Kansas City and rejoined Count Basie.

In 1943, Young was based in New York City—as much as an itinerant jazz man could be based anywhere—and it was inevitable that he would end up playing with the Holy Trinity of Bebop: Charlie Parker, Dizzy Gillespie, and Thelonious Monk. But Young liked to play slow, smooth, and soft. The erratic, faster, and louder sounds of bebop didn't appeal to him, so it was back to Basie again. Ten months later, quirky, quiet Lester Young got drafted into the U.S. Army. To say army life didn't appeal to the sensitive saxophone player would be an understatement. While the military let Benny Goodman and Dave Brubeck entertain the troops, Young didn't get the same treatment. He wasn't even allowed to play his saxophone. An army psychiatrist evaluated Young as "a constitutional psychopath."

While on a military base in Alabama, Young was caught with marijuana and barbiturates. He was put in military prison for almost a year and then kicked out of the service with a dishonorable discharge. Some jazz historians have theorized that the real reason the military was so tough on Young was that he had a common-law wife who was white. Considering the time and place, this is a pretty good theory. And once he was out, he never talked about the military again.

Just as boring punk historians like to debate who the best singer of Black Flag was, boring jazz historians like to debate whether Young's playing got better or worse after his brief military career. From what I have heard, I like the post-army stuff better. The counterargument is that when he was out of the military, his consumption of alcohol greatly increased, diminishing his skills. His drinking definitely took a toll on his health, but we'll let the jazz historians argue online about playing ability.

After World War II, Young found himself in the company of Billie Holiday. They played and recorded together several times and adored each other, but the relationship remained platonic. Holiday was always involved with one human turd or another, and Young burned through a trio of wives in short order. But in 1951, the two friends had a falling-out after a gig in Philadelphia. Young begged Holiday to take it easy on the heroin, and she cut him off for three years. They reunited in 1954 and played together again. But when Young died, his family refused to let Holiday sing at the service. Holiday said, "Those motherfuckers won't let me sing for Prez." She died four months later.

Around 1952, Young was finally leading his own groups and making his own records, though he'd occasionally do a little sideman work. But by the mid-1950s, Young's drinking sent his physical and mental health into crisis mode. He had a nervous breakdown and spent some time recovering in Bellevue Psychiatric Hospital, the same place Charles Mingus would go within a year.

Bellevue was a good rest for Young and 1956 was a productive year for him. He made some fine records, toured Europe, and got some late-career respect. But he was still drinking too much and eating poorly. In 1957, he was hospitalized for alcoholism, malnutrition, and epilepsy. The doctors also discovered cirrhosis and an untreated case of syphilis. Young spent the last couple of years of his life living in a seedy hotel with a view of Birdland, getting fucked up with Billie Holiday.

Young toured Europe again in the spring of 1959. He drank constantly and barely ate. A couple of days before the tour ended, he suffered extreme stomach pains. On the flight back to New York, he vomited blood. He'd broken a vein in his esophagus. After the long, excruciating trans-Atlantic flight, instead of seeking medical attention, the 49-year-old retired to his dingy hotel room and finished drinking himself to death that very night.

WHAT TO CHECK OUT:

The President (1954)

Lester Young with the Oscar Peterson Trio (1954)

The Jazz Giants '56 (1956)

The Lester Young Story (1959)

The Kansas City Sessions (1961)

10 Starters

If you are ready to dip into jazz, here are some of my must-haves. The sweet spot for me is the mid-1950s to the mid-1960s, as you may have noticed, and I like horns. Most of the people I talk jazz with have similar tastes.

Some of these titles I didn't pick up until a few years into my jazz quest. I wish I'd heard them earlier, as they lay a strong foundation for everything else. A baseline, if you will, as opposed to a bass line.

Usually when I try to get into a new artist or genre, I work chronologically. The Ramones, for example, should be experienced in order. But with jazz, I found the titles haphazardly, all out of order, and decades too late. Having no kind of guidance or game plan, I took what I could get when I saw it. My scattershot discovery process muddied my comprehension of the genre. After a few years, the pieces of the jazz puzzle started to fall into place, but there were—and are— still lots of gaps. Researching this book made things a lot clearer.

So, start with anything on this list and work through it in whatever order makes sense. These are landmark recordings, like *Fresh Fruit for Rotting Vegetables* and *Los Angeles*, and are easy to find. One of them is bound to be a new favorite. The late recording engineer SPOT was once asked, "What's your favorite kind of music?" His answer, "Anything I haven't heard," is something I like to keep in mind.

Miles Davis *Kind of Blue* (1959)

John Coltrane *A Love Supreme* (1965)

Charles Mingus *Mingus Ah Um* (1959)

Eric Dolphy *Out to Lunch!* (1964)

Ornette Coleman *The Shape of Jazz to Come* (1959)

Art Blakey and the Jazz Messengers *Moanin'* (1958)

Lee Morgan *The Sidewinder* (1964)

Sonny Rollins *The Bridge* (1962)

Cannonball Adderley *Somethin' Else* (1958)

Chet Baker *Chet Baker Sings* (1954)

THE LAST THING

Punk rock has a huge, diverse family tree, and you probably don't like everything. I don't like much pop punk beyond the first three Screeching Weasel albums. One or two songs is my limit with Oi! and then I need something faster and smarter. My current tolerance for grindcore is about 60 seconds or four songs.

Consider the Grandma Test. If you were to play for your grandma the Sex Pistols, followed by Flipper, followed by Extreme Noise Terror, and told her they were all punk, you'd have a very confused grandma. Grandma would wonder how punk rock got from Point A to Point B to Point C. She might even stop sending you birthday money.

Jazz has an even bigger, more diverse family tree that has been around more than twice as long as punk. Jazz was about 60 years old when the first Ramones album came out!

Consider the Niece Dakota Test. If you were to play for your niece Dakota the Original Dixieland Jass Band, followed by some Kansas City bebop, followed by *Bitches Brew*, and told her they were all jazz, she'd probably make fun of you on TikTok and get a million views in a few hours.

I think the point I am trying to make is if you pick up a jazz recording and don't like it, it doesn't mean you don't like jazz. It means you don't like that record. There are dozens of styles and thousands of artists and tens of thousands of recordings, and at least one of them is bound to make you say, "Whooo—eee! That new music makes me feel like I'm gonna JASM!"

SUGGESTED READING

Beneath the Underdog: His World as Composed by Mingus by Charles Mingus

Billie Holiday by Stuart Nicholson

Billie Holiday: The Musician and the Myth by John Szwed

Bird: The Legend of Charlie Parker by Robert Reisner

Blue Note Records: The Biography by Richard Cook

But Beautiful: A Book About Jazz by Geoff Dyer

Deep in a Dream: The Long Night of Chet Baker by James Gavin

It Wasn't All Velvet: An Autobiography by Mel Tormé

Kansas City Lightning: The Rise and Times of Charlie Parker by Stanley Crouch

Lady Sings the Blues by Billie Holiday and William Dufty

Lester Leaps In: The Life and Times of Lester "Pres" Young by Douglas Henry Daniels

Miles: The Autobiography by Miles Davis and Quincy Troupe

Of Minnie the Moocher & Me by Cab Calloway and Bryant Rollins

Space Is the Place: The Lives and Times of Sun Ra by John Szwed

The Rough Guide to Jazz by Ian Carr

Traps—The Drum Wonder: The Life of Buddy Rich by Mel Tormé

Why Jazz Happened by Marc Myers